D1733414

Having Sex with Your Boyfriend

A Biblical Study of Fornication – The Devastating and Eternal Consequences of Sexual Sin and How to be Delivered

Charlie Avila

The material in this book was developed through nearly forty years of study on the subject and dealing with it on a practical level in the church locally, nationally, and internationally.

Clovis Christian Center
3606 N. Fowler Ave
Fresno, California, USA 93727-1124

ISBN: **9798411254822**
(Softcover Edition)

Printed in the United States

TABLE OF CONTENTS

DEDICATION

This book is affectionately dedicated to Russell Willingham. He has shown both Christians and non-Christians the biblical truths of sexual sin while demonstrating a compassionate love for strugglers. We greatly appreciate his boldness, courage, and leadership in dealing with sexual issues in our day. Thank you.

PREFACE

This important book is about the devastating and eternal consequences of sexual sin. Specifically, we look at the sin of fornication – sex between boyfriend and girlfriend.

First, we define the exact meaning of "fornication." It is a word that is not used very often these days, even among Christians. What does it mean? Where did the word originate? Why does the New Greek Testament use a word that means "to act like a prostitute," "porneuō," to define "fornication" or "sexual immorality?"

In this book, we are going to carefully examine every main verse on "fornication" or "sexual immorality" in the New Testament. The Bible gives a lot of instruction against sexual sin and how to avoid it or repent of it.

We start with the Lord Jesus Christ, the One who is the Truth. Jesus said that fornication – sex between boyfriend and girlfriend – is evil and it defiles people. He exposes the root of the sin and shows its damaging effect on anyone who engages in it.

No one spoke about sexual sin as much as the apostle Paul. He taught against it in Galatians, Ephesians, Colossians, and 1 Thessalonians. However, it is in 1 Corinthians that he lays down a powerful revelation of just how corrupting sexual sin can be for both Christians and non-Christians. Without hesitation, Paul says repeatedly that fornicators go to hell. No sexually immoral man or woman will ever inherit the kingdom of God or Christ.

Interestingly, the one book of the New Testament that says the most about sexual sin is the book of Revelation. Several chapters are from this critical prophetic book. The most corrupting influence in world history has been the great prostitute of Revelation. She is both a city (Babylon) and a woman (the great whore). The kings of the earth and all the inhabitants of the world fornicate with this woman who is "the mother of all harlots (fornicators) and abominations of the earth."

From the book of Hebrews, we learn that all fornicators and adulterers are judged by God. Surprisingly, the author of Hebrews says that all sexually immoral people are like Esau. These are people who sacrifice all of their future and valuable possessions for a few moments of sinful pleasure. Esau and fornicators never gain back what they lose.

In one hard-hitting verse after another, the New Testament writers reveal that believers in Christ are to "flee from fornication," "abstain from fornication," "avoid fornication," "repent of fornication," and "don't commit fornication" because it is "a work of the flesh" that must be "put to death." This sin is so contagious, we are told to have no fellowship with any fornicator – don't even eat lunch with such a person. Paul said that sexual immorality is so deadly, 23,000 of God's people died in one day because of it!

It is the will of God that we live a holy life and abstain from all sexual sin. My body was not made for fornication, but for the Lord. Your body is God's dwelling place. "Do you not know that you are the temple of God and that the Spirit of God dwells in you? Do you not know that your body is the temple of the Holy Spirit who is in you, whom you have from God, and you are not your own?"

My sincere prayer is that all true believers in Christ will read this book and receive its convicting and sanctifying message. Sexual sin is destroying our culture. Let it not destroy you. By the power of the Spirit and the grace of Almighty God, you can live a sexually pure life.

Jesus Christ is Lord. To God be the glory.
Charlie Avila, April 2022

1

What is Fornication?

*Fornication – Having sexual intercourse
with someone to whom one is not married.
(Dictionary Definition)*

I will use the words "fornication," "fornicator," and "committing fornication" in this important book. These words are not commonly used today. What do they mean? Where did they originate? How did we get them into our language?

Like so many English and Spanish words, the word, "fornication," came from the Latin language. A "fornix" was a Roman arch (pictured) that was part of a city gate or an entrance into a certain section of the city (like Rome). In fact, in anatomy, there is an arch-shaped bundle of nerve fibers in the brain that carry signals from the  hippocampus to other parts of the brain including the thalamus and the mammillary bodies. This arch is called a "fornix." Doctors are not certain what it does, but it appears to be part of our memory system.

So, what do Roman arches have to do with sexual immorality? Well, prostitutes in Rome used to stand beneath these building arches and solicit their services. You could find the prostitute under the fornix and indulge in sex with her at some convenient location. This is how we got our word for "fornication." It was from under a "fornix" that you could hire a prostitute and go fornicate.

You may think this is simply an interesting discussion in Latin word origins, but you should also consider Greek word origins. Greek is the language of the New Testament.

When the New Testament writers used the word "harlot" or "prostitute" as in "Rahab the *harlot*" or "Babylon the Great, the Mother of *Harlots*,"[1] they used the word, "pornē." This word comes from a Greek verb that means "to buy." A "pornē" was "a purchased woman." You could buy her for sex. Thus, when the New Testament wants to use any form of the word "fornicate," it will use the Greek word for "harlot," or "pornē," as the root word. Consequently, we see words like "porneia" (fornication), "porneuō" (commit fornication)," or "pornos" (fornicator). Our modern translations often use the words, "sexual immorality." Literally from the Greek, when a girl "commits fornication," she is "acting like a prostitute." That's not difficult to figure out. If you are having sex with your boyfriend, you are doing the same thing a prostitute would do. The only difference is she's getting paid for her services! And yes, the Greek word, "pornos," is where we get our English word for "pornography."[2]

Do you remember what Paul wrote in 1 Corinthians 6:15-16? "Do you not know that your bodies are members of Christ Himself? Shall I then take

---

[1] See Hebrews 11:31, James 2:25, and Revelation 17:5.

[2] This word means "pornos" (harlot) + "graphē" (writing). It is literally, "the writings of a harlot."

the members of Christ and unite them with a prostitute? Never! Do you not know that he who unites himself with a prostitute is one with her in body? For it is said, 'The two will become one flesh.'" Paul gave this instruction to teach us to "flee fornication" (6:18). Yes, there were many shrines and temples in the city of Corinth, including the most famous temple dedicated to Aphrodite, the "goddess of love." The worshippers made free use of the 1,000 consecrated prostitutes at the Temple of Aphrodite. By using the word, "pornē" (harlot), Paul was not necessarily referring to a literal prostitute working the street or at the temple. He was talking about sexual immorality of any kind. We know this is true because in just a few verses he will command[3] them to "get married" because there is "so much sexual immorality" (7:2). Paul was not commanding the Corinthians to marry one of the temple prostitutes just because they had sex with one of them; no, he was referring to the ongoing sexual immorality between people involved with someone they knew (like a girlfriend).

In summary, when you are having sex with your boyfriend or girlfriend, you are fornicating; that is, you are acting just like a prostitute. That is the correct definition of the word from the Latin and Greek languages. And this confirms the definition found in English dictionaries: "To fornicate – Sexual intercourse outside of marriage; sexual intercourse between a man and a woman who are not married, or any form of sexual behavior considered to be immoral."

In the next chapter, let's see what the Lord Jesus said about having sex with your boyfriend or girlfriend.

YouTube Video: **Having Sex With Your Boyfriend 01**

---

[3] Paul uses a Greek imperative verb of command, "echetō," or "let him have!" a wife or husband.

3

HAVING SEX WITH YOUR BOYFRIEND

2

Fornication is Evil and it Defiles You

"What comes out of a man, that defiles a man. For from within, out of the heart of men, proceed evil thoughts, adulteries, fornications, murders, thefts, covetousness, wickedness, deceit, lewdness, an evil eye, blasphemy, pride, foolishness. All these evil things come from within and defile a man."
(Mark 7:20-23)

I will never forget the young teenager who began to attend our church with her family. She was only sixteen. She had a very pretty face and a beautiful, shapely body.

Unfortunately, she began to dress completely inappropriately for the Sunday services. She wore blouses with a plunging neckline and you could see half of her breasts. She also wore very tight jeans. She dressed very provocatively.

Her dad rarely came to the services, but her mother was a regular attender. I decided to talk to her. I talked to one of the ladies in our church – a good friend

5

of the mother – and asked her to join me following a service in one of the Sunday School classrooms where we could meet privately with the mother only. I wanted a friend of hers present so she could feel some moral support.

I wrote 1 Timothy 2:9 on a 3 X 5 card and gave it to the mom. It reads, "And I want women to be modest in their appearance. They should wear decent and appropriate clothing and not draw attention to themselves by the way they fix their hair or by wearing gold or pearls or expensive clothes."

I tried to be very kind and gracious in my words. We wanted them to attend our church but her daughter was inappropriately dressed. The mother blushed. I could see that she was immediately offended. She did not say very much. I said that I would pray for everyone involved and I dismissed the meeting.

The family never came back to our church.

About three months later, I heard that the daughter was pregnant. At the time we met with the mother, she was already having sexual intercourse with her boyfriend. By the end of the year, I had heard that the sixteen-year-old daughter had the baby. I never heard from them again.

Fornication breaks up relationships. It brings shame, guilt, and offenses. It can cause unmarried teenage girls to get pregnant.

More often than not, when I teach on a subject or do a series of messages, I like to start with Jesus. He is "the Truth" and everything He said is true. Did He say anything about "fornication?" Yes, Jesus addressed this critical subject.

Notice what Jesus said in Mark 7:20-23 – "What comes out of a man, that defiles a man. For from within, out of the heart of men, proceed evil thoughts, adulteries, *fornications*, murders, thefts, covetousness, wickedness, deceit, lewdness, an evil eye, blasphemy, pride, foolishness. All these evil things come from within and defile a man."[4]

Jesus said at least three things here about having sex with your boyfriend.

First, the Lord said that fornication is evil. Whether you are in bed somewhere or in the back seat of a car, you are doing something that Jesus considers evil. He concluded by saying, "All these *evil* things…" Jesus also spoke about "*evil* thoughts" and an "*evil* eye." It's a scary thought that Jesus listed "fornications" between "adulteries" and "murders." No one can deny that "murder" is evil.

The word used here for "evil" means "something that is malicious or vicious in its effect and influence." Barclay writes, "*Ponēria* (evil) not only corrupts the person who has it; it corrupts others too. *Ponēros* – the evil one – is the title of Satan. The worst people of all, those who are doing Satan's work, are those who, being bad themselves, make others as bad as they are."[5]

When you have sex with your boyfriend, you are doing what is evil. You are corrupting him; he is corrupting you.

Second, having sex with your boyfriend defiles you. Jesus mentioned it twice – "that defiles a man" and "they defile a man." He said in verse 15, "There is nothing that enters a man from outside which can defile him; but the things which come out of him, those are the things that defile a man." It's not from without but from within.

---

[4] The parallel passage is found in Matthew 15:16-20.
[5] *The Gospel of Mark*, William Barclay, *The New Daily Study Bible*, Westminster John Know, Louisville, Kentucky, page 201. Italics are his.

"To defile" means that you become corrupt. It ruins you. It damages your reputation and good name. It destroys your sanctity. It makes you dirty and pollutes your mind and spirit. If you are a Christian and you're having sexual intercourse with your boyfriend, you've turned your body from being holy and sacred to being unholy and unclean. We'll say more about this in a later chapter when we show how fornicators are like Esau.

Have you noticed how people use dishes, bowls, cups, and glasses in the kitchen? Whenever you want a clean dish or glass, you reach for them from the cupboard. You don't get a glass from the pile of dirty dishes in the sink. Those dishes and glasses must be washed and cleaned first before they can be used. People don't use dirty glasses; they use clean ones.

Do you remember what Paul told Timothy in 2 Timothy 2:20-21? "But in a great house there are not only vessels of gold and silver, but also of wood and clay, some for honor and some for dishonor. Therefore if anyone cleanses himself from the latter, he will be a vessel for honor, sanctified and useful for the Master, prepared for every good work." A paraphrased translation of the last verse reads, "If you keep yourself pure, you will be a special utensil for honorable use. Your life will be clean, and you will be ready for the Master to use you for every good work." The next verse says, "Run from anything that stimulates youthful lusts."

When you're having sex with your boyfriend, you are now in the dirty dish pile. The Master (Jesus) can't use you. You must repent, confess your sin, and be restored. As long as you're fornicating, you cannot be used in the Master's service.

Third, Jesus says that "fornication comes from the heart." So many people think that sexual sins begin by looking at a Playboy magazine, watching pornography on the Internet, or staring at a scantily-clad lady. No, sexual sin begins in the heart. In Mark 7:21, Jesus said, "For from within, *out of the heart of men*, proceed evil thoughts, adulteries, *fornications...*" Adultery (sex outside of marriage) and fornication (sex before marriage) come from the heart. They both start with "evil thoughts." All sexual sin begins with an evil thought.

The biggest sex organ is not between your legs but between your ears. Fornication always begins with "evil thoughts." Before a young man had sex with his girlfriend in bed, he already had sex with her in his mind. Hurtado writes, "The seat of sin and true impurity is the inner area of human intentions and thoughts."[6] Jesus said it this way about adultery in Matthew 5:28 – "I say to you that whoever looks at a woman to lust for her has already committed adultery with her *in his heart*." Jesus forever changed the location of where these sins would be committed. Fornication always begins in the mind and works its way out into the body.

You must take your thoughts captive before they take you captive. Paul wrote in 2 Corinthians 10:4-5, "For the weapons of our warfare are not carnal but mighty in God for pulling down strongholds, casting down arguments and every high thing that exalts itself against the knowledge of God, bringing every thought into captivity to the obedience of Christ."

In the next chapter, we'll see that one of the best ways to handle sexual immorality is to run. Some sins are so deadly, the only way to deal with them is to flee.

YouTube Video: **Having Sex With Your Boyfriend 02**

---

[6] *Mark*, Larry W. Hurtado, New International Biblical Commentary, Hendrickson Publishers, Peabody, Massachusetts, page 111.

HAVING SEX WITH YOUR BOYFRIEND

3

Run From Fornication

*"Flee from fornication. Every sin that a
man does is outside the body; but he that
commits fornication sins against his own
body."*
(1 Corinthians 6:18)

In his insightful little book, *Overcoming
Temptation*, Christian author Don Baker
makes these powerful declarations about
temptation: "Temptation is the method Satan uses to
arouse, to entice, and to persuade us to do something that
God has told us not to do. It's the method the enemy uses
when he wants to destroy a life, a family, a church, a job,
or a reputation. Temptation is a simple method that takes
what is wrong and makes it look right. It takes what is
bad and makes it look good. It takes what is dangerous
and makes it look harmless. Temptation's ultimate goal
is to destroy."[7]

Write this down in your heart: *Satan will tempt
you to have sexual intercourse with your boyfriend or*

---

[7] *Overcoming Temptation*, Don Baker, Harvest House
Publishers, Eugene, Oregon, pages 17-18.

girlfriend because he wants to destroy your life. Fornication is so deadly that Paul says the best way to deal with it is to run. In this case, running is not a sign of weakness, but a sign of strength. One translation of 1 Corinthians 6:18 reads, "Run from sexual sin! No other sin so clearly affects the body as this one does. For sexual immorality is a sin against your own body."

In this verse, Paul used a very strong Greek imperative verb of command, "pheugete!" Run! Escape! Flee! This sin is so deadly, you should not try to stand against it and fight. Take off! Run away! When you're tempted to have sex with your boyfriend, find the nearest exit and run as fast as you can! Morris writes, "The present imperative verb indicates the habitual action or 'Make it your habit to flee.'"[8] Gordon Fee translates it "keep running from" and Blomberg says "to keep on fleeing porneia."[9] This will not be a one-time occurrence. You must keep at it. Don't give in.

When you fornicate with your boyfriend, you are sinning against your own body. You are defiling the temple of the Holy Spirit. You are sinning against a holy God. So much is at stake. Satan wants to destroy you. In a later chapter, we'll cover 1 Corinthians 10:8: "We should not commit sexual immorality (porneuō), as some of them did – and in one day twenty-three thousand of them died." *Thousands of God's people died because of fornication.* Thousands! Died! We'll also cover Hebrews 13:4, "But fornicators and adulterers God will judge." You're going to dishonor marriage. You're going to defile the marriage bed. You're going to be judged by God!

---

[8]   *1 Corinthians*, Leon Morris, Tyndale New Testament Commentaries, Revised Edition, Eerdmans Publishing, Grand Rapids, Michigan, page 98.

[9] See *The First Epistle to the Corinthians*, Gordon D. Fee, page 260 and *1 Corinthians*, Craig Blomberg, page 129.

Paul commanded Timothy to "flee youthful lusts," "flee the evil desires of youth," or "run from anything that stimulates youthful lusts."[10] Paul would command the Corinthians to "flee idolatry." He would also tell Timothy to "flee covetousness" or "flee the love of money."[11] These sins are so deadly, the only thing you can do is run!

There was a man in the Bible who ran. His name was Joseph. He was Jacob's son. His story is found in Genesis, Chapter 39.

Potiphar, the captain of Pharaoh's guard, bought Joseph as a slave. The text tells us that "the Lord was with Joseph, and he was a successful man" (39:2). "The Lord made all he did to prosper in his hand" (39:3). "Joseph found favor in Potiphar's sight," and Potiphar made him "overseer of all his house" (39:4). "The Lord even blessed the Egyptian's house for Joseph's sake; and the blessing of the Lord was on all that he had in the house and in the field" (39:5). On top of all that, "Joseph was handsome in form and appearance" (39:6).

There was one big problem in the midst of all this success – Joseph found himself all alone with Potiphar's wife and she tempted him. *Never forget: You will always be tempted to sexual sin whenever you are all alone with someone of the opposite sex. Always!*

I love Baker's words: "Potiphar's wife was the perfect complement to a husband on the rise. She was beautiful, exciting, gracious, and witty. But she was bored, and she was lonely and she was neglected and she was resentful. Then she met Joseph. Joseph was handsome and sensitive and efficient and attentive and far from home and thirty and he was there."

Baker continues: "Each morning, Joseph assumed his duties managing the affairs of Potiphar. And

---

[10] See 2 Timothy 2:22.
[11] See 1 Corinthians 10:14; 1 Timothy 6:11.

each day Joseph listened attentively to the frustrations of Potiphar's wife. Then it happened. This young, exciting, lonely, and neglected housewife saw the solution to her problem of loneliness in the young, handsome, sensitive, and attentive manager of her husband's affairs.

One day when Potiphar was gone and Potiphar's wife was feeling especially lonely, Joseph entered to perform his usual duties. Joseph and Potiphar's wife talked and they talked and they talked until, without warning, she said with characteristic modern-day boldness, 'Come to bed with me.'

Joseph wanted God's blessing and Potiphar's respect even more than he wanted Potiphar's wife.

Then, suddenly, the lonely wife of an ambitious husband reached for the buttons of Joseph's shirt.

This was not the time for reason or resistance or resignation. It was time to run. Joseph ran.

To some, running away may seem to be the act of a coward, but running was a mark of great spiritual strength.

And in today's sensuous culture, running is probably the best way to resist temptation."[12]

Never find yourself alone in an apartment with your boyfriend or girlfriend. Don't find yourself alone in a car in a secluded place at some park. You're going to start kissing and touching and taking clothes off. Sexual passion burns like a raging fire. You won't be able to stop. You won't be able to resist.

Blomberg's comments are appropriate here about fleeing fornication: "It may require refusing intimate friendships with people to whom one is improperly attracted; refraining in dating relationships from bodily contact that prematurely arouses too strong a sexual desire; or avoiding places that make pornography

---

[12] *Overcoming Temptation*, pages 11-16.

available in print or on television or film."[13] The greatest area of temptation today is the Internet! So many people, including Christians, are falling into sexual sin at the click of a mouse or the touch of a screen.

When you are tempted to sin sexually against God and your friend, run! Flee! Escape!

There is a way you can have sexual intercourse with your boyfriend: Get married. That is the subject of the next chapter.

YouTube Video: **Having Sex With Your Boyfriend 03**

---

[13] *1 Corinthians*, Blomberg, page 129.

HAVING SEX WITH YOUR BOYFRIEND

4

If You want to have Sex, Get Married

"Because there is so much sexual immorality, each man should have his own wife, and each woman should have her own husband."
(1 Corinthians 7:2)

"If they cannot control themselves, they should marry, for it is better to marry than to burn with passion."
(1 Corinthians 7:9)

Sexual intercourse is the exclusive domain of marriage. In God's sight, the only sex that is pure and holy is that between a married man and his wife. Any sex before marriage, outside of marriage, or between people of the same sex is a perversion of God's original design. When a woman has sex with her boyfriend, she is fornicating with him and sinning against the Lord. When a married man has sex with another married woman, he is committing adultery and violating one of God's Ten Commandments. When someone – regardless of marital status – has sex with another person of the same sex, this is homosexuality. It is an abomination in God's eyes.

If you are a Christian believer, and you want to have sex with your boyfriend or girlfriend, you need to get married *first*. The Lord only permits sexual intercourse between a man and a woman who are married.

Very importantly, you should not marry someone just to have sex. You should marry another person because he's a Christian. You should marry because it's God's will for your life. You should marry because you have true agape love for him or her. You should get married by your Pastor in a wedding ceremony after some premarital counseling.

Don't elope.[14] Don't run off so you can start having sex. Don't run to the nearest wedding chapel and pay a few dollars so you can get married on the same day. Do it God's way. Do it right. Don't cheapen the marriage covenant. Get the confirmation of your family, parents, friends, Pastor, and church leaders. Have a wedding and invite your family and friends. I've seen so many "overnight" marriages fail because the couple exercised no patience, no self-control, and no waiting on the Lord. Don't do it this way!

In 1 Corinthians 7:1, Paul writes literally in Greek: "It is good for a man not to touch a woman." "To touch a woman" is a Greek euphemism[15] for "have sexual

---

[14] "Elope" is defined as "to leave secretly to get married: to go away suddenly without telling anyone, especially in order to marry or cohabit with a lover without the knowledge or consent of parents or guardians." It comes from an Anglo-Norman word, "aloper," which means "to run away."

[15] A "euphemism" is "a word or phrase used in place of a term that might be considered too direct, harsh, unpleasant, or offensive."

relations with a woman."[16] Don't have sex with a (single) woman. The NCV reads, "It is good for a man not to have sexual relations with a woman." It is a good thing to abstain from sex until you get married.

We see this use of "touching a woman" in Proverbs 6:29 when Solomon talks about adultery: "So is he who goes in to his neighbor's wife; whoever *touches* her shall not be innocent." Also, when Abimelech took Abraham's wife, Sarah, into his harem of women, the Lord kept him from having sex with her: "God said to him in a dream, 'Yes, I know that you did this in the integrity of your heart. For I also withheld you from sinning against Me; therefore, I did not let you *touch* her.'"[17]

Again, "To not touch a woman" meant to not have sexual relations with a single woman.

I want to say something here about physical touch. If you and your boyfriend start spending a lot of time alone kissing and touching each other physically, you are not far away from fornicating. It will naturally lead to sexual intercourse. You will not be able to stop it. The fire has started and it will not be quenched until you begin having sex. This is always a guilt-ridden, shame-filled episode in the life of two Christian singles.

1 Corinthians 7:2 says, "Because there is so much sexual immorality, each man should have his own wife, and each woman should have her own husband." Paul now gives one of the reasons why people should marry – "Because there is so much sexual immorality" or "because sexual sin is a danger." As a Christian single, you will be tempted to sin sexually. In 1 Corinthians 7:9, Paul will say that "it's better to marry than to burn with passion." Before and after marriage, "self-control" is a big issue. *Before marriage, you need self-control so you*

---

[16] See the United Bible Society (UBS) Translators' Handbook on 1 Corinthians, especially their notes on 7:1.
[17] See Genesis 20:6.

don't commit fornication; after marriage, you need self-control so you don't commit adultery (7:5).

Paul uses the verbs "let have" and "let have" in 7:2 (twice). They are both Greek imperative verbs of command. He insists on getting married to deal with all the "sexual immorality." It's better to get married and engage in sexual intercourse with a wife than with your girlfriend next door, or in the case of the Corinthians, with the local prostitute down at the pagan temple.

However, as most of us know, marriage doesn't usually solve our sex problems. In fact, most people who are regularly viewing pornography, masturbating, or watching sexually explicit movies are married (men and women). Often, marriage doesn't solve our sexual needs.

Here is another thing you should never do with your boyfriend: After you've set a wedding date, don't rationalize in your mind that you're getting married in a few weeks anyway, so let's start having sex now. Don't do this. Honor the Lord. Obey the Word of God. Both of you should be virgins when you stand before the minister on wedding day to say your vows. Let your wedding night be a special night of consummation and covenant love.

1 Corinthians 7:3 (NLT) reads, "The husband should fulfill his wife's sexual needs, and the wife should fulfill her husband's needs." It does not say, "The boyfriend should fulfill his girlfriend's sexual needs" and vice versa. Again, only sex between a married man and his wife is permitted by the Lord.

We know that Paul was talking about sexual intercourse in verse 3 because of what he writes in verse 4. This body, that is the temple of the Holy Spirit (6:19-20), also belongs to your husband. He has "authority over" his wife's body. Likewise, the wife has authority over the husband's body. Bruce writes, "By the marriage vow each relinquishes the exclusive right to his or her own body and gives the other a claim to it."[18] Only in marriage can the body be surrendered. As a single person, your body does not belong to your boyfriend. It belongs to the Lord. Only when you get married can you exercise this "authority over" the body of your husband or your wife.

Single Christian man, always keep in mind that your girlfriend's body is the temple of the Holy Spirit. Her body must be treated with holiness and respect because God's Spirit dwells in her. In 1 Corinthians 7:34, it says, "The unmarried woman cares about the things of the Lord, that she may be holy both in body and in spirit." Your girlfriend is to keep, not just her spirit, but "her body" holy before the Lord. Don't violate her holiness by fornicating with her.

In the next chapter, we'll see that your body was not made for sexual immorality, but for the Lord. Your body was not made to satisfy perverted sexual appetites but to serve and worship the Lord in love.

YouTube Video: **Having Sex With Your Boyfriend 04**

---

[18] *1 & 2 Corinthians*, F. F. Bruce, The New Century Bible Commentary, Eerdmans Publishing Company, Grand Rapids, MI, page 67.

HAVING SEX WITH YOUR BOYFRIEND

5

Your Body was Made for the Lord

*"Now the body is not for sexual immorality
but for the Lord, and the Lord for the body."
(1 Corinthians 6:13)*

In this important verse – 1 Corinthians 6:13 – you learn a fundamental truth: *Your body was not made for sexual immorality; it was made for the Lord.* At the end of this chapter, Paul writes, "For you were bought at a price; therefore glorify God in your body and in your spirit, which are God's" (v20). You belong to God. Your body is a member of the body of Christ. Your body is the temple of the Holy Spirit. As a Christian believer, you belong to Jesus Christ Himself!

When you buy a glove, you do not put it on your ear. You don't put it on your foot. A glove was made for the hand and the hand for the glove.

In the same way, Paul says at the beginning of 6:13, "Food for the stomach and the stomach for food." You don't put food in your ear. You can't feed yourself through your nose. The only part of the body that was made specifically for food is your stomach.

The glove is for the hand. Food is for the body. So, your body is for the Lord. It was not made so you could sin sexually against the Lord. *Don't use your body to sin against the Lord; use your body to serve the Lord!* You're free to serve the Lord, not the flesh.

The Corinthians thought "fornication was as natural as eating. But God did not design the body for sexual immorality as He did the stomach for food."[19]

The Greek word that the apostle used here in verse 13 for "sexual immorality" is "porneia," literally "to be a prostitute." As a verb, it means "to act like a prostitute." God did not give you a body so you could sin against Him.

God's glorious future plans for your physical body are detailed in the next verse: "God both raised up the Lord and will also raise us up by His power (v14)." God raised Jesus with a new, glorified body. At the final resurrection, you will also get this new, glorified body.[20] It is a body that will never again sin, get sick, or suffer!

Wiersbe says, "He created our bodies and one day He will resurrect them in glory. In view of the fact that our bodies have such a wonderful origin, and an even more wonderful future, how can we use them for such evil purposes?" This is true. God created our magnificent bodies just for Him. The future destiny of your body is not destruction, but resurrection. "The resurrection forbids us to take the body lightly."[21] So, don't use it now to fornicate with your boyfriend.

Let's follow Jesus' own example. Why was He given a physical body? Hebrews 10:5 reads, "A body

---

[19] *1 Corinthians*, Leon Morris, Tyndale New Testament Commentaries, Eerdmans Publishing, Grand Rapids, Michigan, page 96.
[20] See verses like Philippians 3:20-21; 1 Corinthians 15:42-44, 53.
[21] *1 Corinthians*, Morris, page 97.

You (God) have prepared for Me." Why? "Behold, I have come to do Your will, O God" (10:7).[22] What a great word for Christians today! God gave you a body so you also could do His will. He didn't give it to you so you could "act like a prostitute!" *Live for the glory of God. Live for the will of God.*

All Christians – including Christian singles – must keep in mind that we will give an account unto God for what we have done in this physical body. In his 2nd letter to the Corinthians, Paul would write, "For we must all appear before the judgment seat of Christ; that every one may receive the things done in his body, according to what he has done, whether it be good or bad."[23] Don't stand before the Lord's judgment seat with your life defiled and stained with fornication. This is "bad."

Let's get back to the fundamental issue of 1 Corinthians 6:13: *Jesus Christ is Lord.* He must be obeyed. His Lordship demands obedience. Your body belongs to Him, not your boyfriend. Your boyfriend is not lord; Jesus is Lord! Give Him your spirit, soul, and body to be used for the glory of God. Surrender to Jesus, not to sexual sin. Schreiner is right: "The word, *Lord*, signals that Jesus is master over one's body; He rules over what believers do with their bodies."[24]

At the end of the day, you are presented with a choice: you can either give yourself to fornication or you can give yourself to the Lord. Your body was made for the Lord. Give Him your body and keep it pure and holy.

---

[22] This is quote from Psalm 40:6-8. There it says of Jesus, "I delight to do Your will, O my God."

[23] See 2 Corinthians 5:10.

[24] *1 Corinthians*, Thomas R. Schreiner, Tyndale New Testament Commentaries, Inter-Varsity Press, Downers Grove, Illinois, page 127.

God provides a way out for those who have been fornicating. The Lord commands that all people repent of fornication. It is a deadly sin that destroys. Repentance is a blessing from God. Let's look at that topic next.

YouTube Video: **Having Sex With Your Boyfriend 05**

6

Repent of Fornication

*"I am afraid that when I come again my
God will humble me before you, and I will
be grieved over many who have sinned
earlier and have not repented of the
impurity, sexual sin and debauchery in
which they have indulged."*
(2 Corinthians 12:21)

The Christian couple had big smiles on their faces. They were ecstatic. "Pastor Charlie, our first grandchild is on the way!" Their son had been fornicating with his girlfriend, and now, she was pregnant with "the love child." They had already made celebratory announcements on social media. This is the new moral standard. This is the new sexual ethos. This is the new perspective of so many Christian believers – Rejoice that your adult children are having sex outside of marriage and getting young girls pregnant out of wedlock.

I was torn. I didn't know how to react. Do I rejoice too? Do I celebrate sexual sin and its dark consequences? Do I ask, "Are they married?" What's the appropriate Christian response? What would Jesus do?

Here in 2 Corinthians 12:21, Paul "mourns," "grieves," "anguishes," or "weeps" because *many* Corinthian believers "have not repented of the uncleanness, fornication (porneia), and lewdness which they have practiced." How did the apostle Paul react? *It struck him as if someone had died.* "Pentheō" was a Greek word used at funerals when a loved one died. It is usually translated as "mourn" or "wailing." It's a deep grief after experiencing a devastating loss.

Paul said that these Christians continued to practice "uncleanness, fornication, and lewdness" – three terms directly associated with sexual immorality and lust. They had given themselves over to lewd and perverted behavior. These believers had "not repented." They kept on indulging in sexual sins without the slightest conviction or qualm. You can probably hear them say: "This is normal...I'm just satisfying my natural sexual desires...this is what it means to be a real man in Corinth...besides, *everybody else is doing it.*"

Having sexual intercourse with your boyfriend and girlfriend sure is exciting, fulfilling, gratifying, pleasurable, and passionate. You've never experienced such an amazing rush and release of energy and obsession. Your wildest desires and strongest appetites are being met by someone you've fallen in love with. How can this be so wrong when it feels so right?

In the midst of such euphoria, you need something very desperately from the Lord. You need His gracious gift of repentance in your heart. You need to repent! As Paul told the Romans, "The goodness of God leads you to repentance."[25] Paul said in 2 Timothy 2:25-26 that there were people "who need to come to their senses" because they have been "taken captive to do the

---

[25] See Romans 2:4.

will" of the flesh and of the devil. "God must grant them repentance so they will acknowledge the truth."

What does "repent" mean? It means to change completely the way you're thinking. Get your mind renewed. You're looking at this all wrong. Your thinking has been corrupted by worldly wisdom and you're heading down the road to destruction.

Don't you see that fornicators end up in the "lake of fire" (Revelation 21:8)? Fornicators are judged by God (Hebrews 13:4). Fornication is a work of the flesh and is at war against the Holy Spirit (Galatians 5:16-19). Fornication is evil and brings the wrath of God (Mark 7:20-23; Colossians 3:5-6). Fornicators are deceived and have no inheritance in the kingdom of God or of Christ (Ephesians 5:5; 1 Corinthians 6:9). Fornication destroys lives and destroys your spiritual life (1 Corinthians 10:8).

Yes, your mind must be renewed and transformed to what the Word of God is saying. Again, "repent" means to have a complete change of mind. Your thinking is all wrong. Paul wrote, "Put to death your members which are on the earth: fornication, uncleanness, passion, evil desire, and covetousness, which is idolatry. Because of these things the wrath of God is coming upon the sons of disobedience, in which you yourselves once walked when you lived in them."[26] Rather than looking for opportunities to sleep with your boyfriend, you should be putting fornication to death!

Yes, it is convenient to live together with your boyfriend. Yes, you will save money on rent. Yes, you'll enjoy the pleasures of sin for a season. Yes, you're going to get married next year…but you are sinning against the Lord. You are grieving the Holy Spirit. You are endangering your life with future curses. What if you

---

[26] See Colossians 3:5-7.

contract a venereal disease? What if your girlfriend gets pregnant? Worse of all, what if that close fellowship you once had with Jesus Christ vanishes? What if that abundant life in Christ turns into a life filled with condemnation, guilt, and shame because you know you're doing what displeases your Lord?

Galatians 6:7-8 reads, "Do not be deceived, God is not mocked; for whatever a man sows, that he will also reap. For he who sows to his flesh will of the flesh reap corruption (destruction), but he who sows to the Spirit will of the Spirit reap everlasting life." Sow to the Spirit!

Get on your knees right now and repent. Turn around. Get right with the Lord. Move out of that apartment. Ask for the Lord's merciful forgiveness.

God has given you a way out. You need to repent!

John the Baptist came preaching: "*Repent*, for the kingdom of heaven is at hand!"

Jesus said, "*Repent*, for the kingdom of heaven is at hand."

The apostles "went out and preached that people should *repent*."

The Lord said, "I have not come to call the righteous, but sinners, to *repentance*."

Don't worry about how others are living. "I tell you, no; but unless you *repent* you will all likewise perish."

On the day of Pentecost, Peter preached, "*Repent* and be baptized, every one of you, in the name of Jesus Christ for the forgiveness of your sins. And you will receive the gift of the Holy Spirit."

The apostle said, "*Repent*, then, and turn to God, so that your sins may be wiped out, and that times of refreshing may come to you from the Lord."

"God is not willing that any should perish but that all should come to *repentance*."

"In the past, God overlooked such ignorance, but now He commands all people everywhere to *repent*."

Jesus told one church, "Remember therefore from where you have fallen; *repent* and do the first works, or else I will come to you quickly and remove your lampstand from its place – unless you *repent*" and another church, "as many as I love, I rebuke and chasten. Therefore be zealous and *repent*."

Stop fornicating and make things right with God. He is commanding you to repent of your sexual immorality and get back on track with Him.

Fornication is a work of the flesh. It is a sin at war with the Holy Spirit of God. Let's go to Galatians and Romans and talk about that next.

YouTube Video: **Having Sex With Your Boyfriend 06**

HAVING SEX WITH YOUR BOYFRIEND

7

Fornication is a Work of the Flesh

"Now the works of the flesh are evident,
which are: adultery, fornication,
uncleanness, and lewdness."
(Galatians 5:19)

Jesus told us that fornication is evil. He also said that it defiles a person. Here in Galatians 5:19, the apostle Paul adds another important element – *Fornication is a work of the flesh.* In this verse, "fornication" is listed along with three other sexual sins – "adultery," "uncleanness," and "lewdness." These sex sins are so serious to Paul that he can conclude two verses later, "…those who practice such things will not inherit the kingdom of God" (v21). In other words, if you are having sex with your boyfriend, and if you don't repent, you will go to hell if you die! We will elaborate on this sobering truth in a few other chapters.

What does the Bible mean when it uses the word, "flesh?" Many times, Paul is simply referring to our physical body. However, here in Galatians 5:19, it means that carnal, sinful, or rebellious nature in people that came

33

as a result of the Fall in the Garden of Eden. When Adam disobeyed the Lord in Genesis Chapter 3, he became a sinner, and his sinful nature was passed on to every person who would ever be born on planet earth. The Bible says, "Just as through one man sin entered the world, and death through sin, and thus death spread to all men, because all sinned" and "by one man's disobedience many were made sinners."[27]

When you are having sex with your girlfriend, you are engaging in lust, and everything about the flesh centers around lust. Sexual lust is that sinful longing, passion, or desire for sex, usually without any associated feelings of love or affection.

Fornication is a fleshly lust. Notice the overwhelming testimony of Scripture: "Make no provision for the *flesh*, to fulfill its *lusts*," "you shall not fulfill the *lust* of the *flesh*...for the *flesh lusts* against the Spirit," "we all once conducted ourselves in the *lusts* of our *flesh*, fulfilling the desires of the *flesh* and of the mind," "abstain from *fleshly lusts* which war against the soul," "that you should no longer live the rest of your time in the *flesh* for the *lusts* of men," "especially those who walk according to the *flesh* in the *lust* of uncleanness," "they allure through the *lusts* of the *flesh*, through lewdness," and "for all that is in the world – the *lust* of the *flesh*, the *lust* of the eyes, and the pride of life – is not of the Father but is of the world."[28] Jesus defined adultery as "whoever looks at a woman to *lust* for her"; Paul said homosexuality involved "men, who left the natural use of the woman, and burned in their *lust* for one another"; and he taught that fornication was "the passion of *lust*" of "the Gentiles." The apostle Peter went so far as to declare that

---

[27] See Romans 5:12 and 5:19.
[28] See Romans 13:14; Galatians 5:16-17; Ephesians 2:3; 1 Peter 2:11, 4:2; 2 Peter 2:10, 2:18; 1 John 2:16.

the "whole world is corrupted through *lust*."[29] Make no mistake about it: *Lust has a worldwide influence.*[30]

When you're having sex with your boyfriend, you can never please God for Romans 8:8 reads, "Those who are in the flesh cannot please God."

When you're having sex with your boyfriend, you are living in death for Romans 8:6 says, "For to be carnally minded is death." The Greek word here for "carnal" (sarx) is the exactly same word translated elsewhere as "flesh." To be carnally minded is to be fleshly minded.

When you're having sex with your girlfriend, your actions are hostile toward God and His laws. You are rebelling against God's will. Romans 8:7 says, "The carnal mind is enmity against God; for it is not subject to the law of God, nor indeed can be." Another translation reads, "For the sinful nature is always hostile to God. It never did obey God's laws, and it never will." For you to continue to have sexual intercourse with your girlfriend is a stubborn act of defiance against a holy God.

Once again, God has provided a way out. He teaches us clearly how to get delivered from fornication.

God's answer for overcoming the enemy of the flesh and its lusts is not a formula, a secret technique, a special seminar, prayer meeting, or a church program, but in a Person – the Person of the Holy Spirit! The Spirit of

---

[29] See Matthew 5:28; Romans 1:27; 1 Thessalonians 4:5; 2 Peter 1:4.

[30] We will speak extensively about this in Chapter 11. In Revelation, John saw the Babylonian prostitute (pornē) as corrupting "all nations" (14:8), "the kings of the earth" and "the inhabitants of the earth" (17:2), "all the nations" and "the kings of the earth" (18:3), "the kings of the earth" (18:9), and "the earth" (19:2) with her fornication. Yes, the whole world is corrupted by fornication!

God is all-powerful, and He alone can sanctify and cleanse you from the fleshly work of fornication.

No doubt, the classic verse is Galatians 5:16: "Walk in the Spirit, and you shall not fulfill the lust of the flesh." No doubt, the classic chapter is Romans 8: "We who do not walk according to the flesh but according to the Spirit" (v4), "for those who live according to the flesh set their minds on the things of the flesh, but those who live according to the Spirit, the things of the Spirit" (v5), "you are not in the flesh but in the Spirit" (v9), "we are debtors – not to the flesh, to live according to the flesh for if you live according to the flesh you will die; but if by the Spirit you put to death the deeds of the body, you will live" (vv12-13). Always keep in mind that the Spirit of God is infinitely more powerful than any fleshly action.

What is the part we play? You have to crucify the flesh. You have to put fornication to death. Galatians 5:24 says, "Those who are Christ's have crucified the flesh with its passions and desires." Colossians 3:5 reads, "Put to death your members which are on the earth: fornication, uncleanness, passion, and evil desire." Do you see the words – "By the Spirit, you put to death," "crucify the flesh," and "put to death your members?" What does this mean? Don't feed it. Don't add fuel to the fire. Don't open a door that has already been closed. This is what Paul meant when he wrote, "Put on the Lord Jesus Christ, and make no provision for the flesh, to fulfill its lusts."[31]

Christians make provision for the flesh all the time. They make room to fulfill its lusts. If you know your girlfriend's parents will be away from the house for the evening, and you make plans to go see her during this time of absence, you're making provision for the flesh. If you're already making plans to be together alone in the

---

[31] See Romans 13:14.

park in a secluded place, you're making provision to fornicate.

Make plans to meet your boyfriend at a restaurant where other people are present. Make plans to meet at a church event or movie theater or sporting event or when his parents are around. This is part of the practical plan of putting fornication to death. When you're all alone, the tempter will tempt you!

The works of the flesh are deadly serious. "For he who sows to his flesh will of the flesh reap corruption."[32] Some translations use "destruction," "ruin," and "eternal death." With fornication, you will reap (harvest) some terrible consequences. When I lived in Ohio, I heard the story of a Christian who was single who died while having sex with his girlfriend! He was only 33 years old. We think it was a heart attack. This news sent shockwaves throughout the singles' groups of our city. Another Christian told me of an incurable sexually transmitted disease that he contracted after having sex with a girlfriend that he hardly knew. Another Christian teenager (19) became pregnant after sex with her unsaved boyfriend in her apartment.

Be warned today Christian single! Your sin will surely find you out.[33] What was done in secret will become known in public.

On this book cover, the subtitle says that fornication is a sin with "eternal consequences." We'll see why that's true in the next chapter. No one who is fornicating will ever be able to enter the kingdom of God.

YouTube Video: **Having Sex With Your Boyfriend 07**

---

[32] See Galatians 6:8.
[33] See Numbers 32:23.

HAVING SEX WITH YOUR BOYFRIEND

8

No Fornicator will Inherit the Kingdom of Christ

*"For this you know, that no fornicator,
unclean person, nor covetous man, who is
an idolater, has any inheritance in the
kingdom of Christ and God. Let no one
deceive you with empty words, for because
of these things the wrath of God comes upon
the sons of disobedience."*
(Ephesians 5:5-6)

There is a question in Galatians 4:16 that has provoked me to much contemplation and reflection. I have mentioned it to many Christian believers over the years. Paul asks, "Have I become your enemy because I tell you the truth?"

What Paul says here in Ephesians Chapter 5 is plain and easy to understand, but it is a very hard truth from God's Word. Paul teaches that *no fornicator will ever make it into heaven. All fornicators go to hell.* Look at the words again – "No fornicator, unclean person, nor covetous man, who is an idolater, has any inheritance in the kingdom of Christ and God" (v5).

Paul is absolutely sure about this truth. One translation of Ephesians 5:5 reads, "You can be sure of this: No one will have a place in the kingdom of Christ and of God if that person commits sexual sins." There are only two eternal destinations – you're either going to the kingdom of God or the lake of fire. There has never been a third place.

Paul is so sure of this that in 1 Corinthians 6:9-10, he writes, "Do you not know that the unrighteous will *not inherit the kingdom of God*? Do not be deceived. Neither *fornicators*, nor idolaters, nor adulterers, nor homosexuals, nor sodomites, nor thieves, nor covetous, nor drunkards, nor revilers, nor extortioners *will inherit the kingdom of God*." Fornicators will not inherit the kingdom of God.

Paul is so sure of this that in Galatians 5:19-21, he writes again, "Now the works of the flesh are evident, which are: adultery, *fornication*, uncleanness, lewdness, idolatry, sorcery, hatred, contentions, jealousies, outbursts of wrath, selfish ambitions, dissensions, heresies, envy, murders, drunkenness, revelries, and the like; of which I tell you beforehand, just as I also told you in time past, *that those who practice such things will not inherit the kingdom of God*." Again, anyone living in fornication will not inherit God's kingdom. You will go to hell. In fact, *anyone living in any type of sexual immorality will go to hell*. The apostle John wrote in Revelation 21:8, "But the cowardly, unbelieving, abominable, murderers, *sexually immoral* (pornos), sorcerers, idolaters, and all liars shall have their part in the lake which burns with fire and brimstone, which is the second death," and in Revelation 22:15, "But outside are dogs and sorcerers and *sexually immoral* (pornoi)[34] and murderers and idolaters, and whoever loves and practices

---

[34] "Pornoi" is the plural form of "pornos."

a lie." The truth is that all unrepentant, sexually immoral people will go into the lake of fire. Fornicators, adulterers, homosexuals, and any others living in sexual sin will suffer eternal damnation! *You can be sure of this*.

Paul had written two verses earlier, in Ephesians 5:3, "But fornication and all uncleanness or covetousness, let it not even be named among you, as is fitting for saints." Another translation says, "But among you there must not be even a hint of sexual immorality, or of any kind of impurity." Still another reads, "Such sins have no place among God's holy people." Fornication should have no place in the Christian's life. Not even a hint, Paul says. This is not right for God's people who are commanded to live a holy life. Christians are called "saints" sixty times in the New Testament. Literally in Greek, this means "the holy ones." No Christian who is fornicating can be walking with a holy God. You are not following the *Holy* Spirit; you are in the flesh.

After commanding Christians to "abstain from fornication," Paul writes, "For God did not call us to uncleanness, but to holiness."[35]

There is so much deception about fornication. So many people think it is okay. This is normal. People rationalize that we have sexual needs, and having sex with your boyfriend is just another way of expressing love to him. But Paul warns in the next verse, in Ephesians 5:6, "Let no one deceive you with empty words." Don't try to justify fornication with vain, empty words. You might say, "But everyone is doing it" or "we're going to get married anyway" or "my parents are okay with it" or "I'm practicing safe sex – I'm using a birth control pill and my boyfriend uses a condom." There's nothing safe about it – you're going to hell! Paul also told the Corinthians, "Do not be deceived" (6:9). Don't deceive yourself!

---

[35] See 1 Thessalonians 4:3 and 4:7. "Uncleanness" here is a sexual term. Just as it is in Ephesians 5:3 and 5:5.

Barclay writes, "There were voices in the ancient world, even in the Christian Church, which taught people to think lightly of the sin of physical desires. The gravest disservice anyone can do to someone else is to make that person take sin lightly. Paul pleaded with his converts not to be deceived with empty words which removed the horror from the idea of sin."[36] If you are a Christian, and you are fornicating, stop making light of sin! The wages of sin is death!

Paul continues in Ephesians 5:6-7: "...for because of these things the wrath of God comes upon the sons of disobedience. Therefore do not be partakers with them." These things – fornication, uncleanness, and covetousness – incite the wrath of God! Some translations speak of "the anger of God" or "God gets very angry." Don't be one of "the sons of disobedience" who makes the Lord angry. Paul told the Colossians, "Put to death fornication, uncleanness, passion, evil desire, and covetousness, which is idolatry. Because of these things the wrath of God is coming upon the sons of disobedience."[37] Make no mistake about it – God's wrath will come upon you! Fornicators will experience it now and they will experience it forever in hell. With a very strong Greek imperative verb of command, Paul says, "Do not be partakers with them!" If you participate in the sins of the wicked, you will also share in their doom.

Instead of living in fornication, what does Paul say in Ephesians 5? He writes, "Walk in love" (5:2), "walk in the light" (5:8) and "walk in wisdom" (5:15). All Christians should be "imitators of God" (5:1), not "partakers" (5:7) of evil. Paul adds, "Have no fellowship with the unfruitful works of darkness, but rather expose

---

[36] *The Letters to the Galatians and Ephesians*, William Barclay, The New Daily Study Bible, John Knox Press, Louisville, Kentucky, pages 187-188.

[37] See Colossians 3:5-6.

them. For it is shameful even to speak of those things which are done by them in secret" (5:11-12). Having sex with your girlfriend is an "unfruitful work of darkness." It is "shameful." It is a "secret sin" that corrupts you.

Paul speaks about "putting fornication to death." What does that mean? That is the subject of the next chapter.

YouTube Video: **Having Sex With Your Boyfriend 08**

HAVING SEX WITH YOUR BOYFRIEND

9

Putting Fornication to Death

*"Put to death your members which are on
the earth: fornication, uncleanness, passion,
evil desire, and covetousness, which is
idolatry. Because of these things the wrath
of God is coming upon the sons of
disobedience."
(Colossians 3:5-6)*

One of the most powerful truths that the
Holy Spirit ever gave to Paul was that
Christians are "dead to sin." When Christ
died, you died. When Christ was crucified, you were
crucified. The old man has been executed when Christ
died on the cross. This truth is very clearly stated by Paul
in his letters.

"How shall we who died to sin live any longer in
it," "that our old man was crucified with Him," "we died
with Christ," "reckon yourselves to be dead indeed to
sin," and "I have been crucified with Christ."[38] Here in
Colossians – the focus of this chapter – Paul writes, "You
died with Christ" (2:20) and "for you died" (3:3).

---

[38] See Romans 6:2, 6:6, 6:8, 6:11 and Galatians 2:20.

Because you are "in Christ," whatever happened to Christ, happened to us. So, we "died to sin" through the cross; we were "buried with Him" through baptism; and we were "raised with Him" through His resurrection from the dead.

And where does sin do its dirty work? It does it through the parts of our body – what Paul calls "our members." Notice Paul's words: "The sinful passions which were aroused by the law were at work *in our members* to bear fruit to death" and "I see another law *in my members*, warring against the law of my mind, and bringing me into captivity to the law of sin which is *in my members*." Our sinful, carnal, fleshly actions manifest themselves through "our members," the parts of the body.

Perhaps the deadliest "member" of your body is your tongue. James 3:5-6 says, "Even so the tongue is a *little member* and boasts great things. See how great a forest a little fire kindles! And the tongue is a fire, a world of iniquity. The tongue is so set *among our members* that it defiles the whole body, and sets on fire the course of nature; and it is set on fire by hell." James will also say, "Where do wars and fights come from among you? Do they not come from your desires for pleasure that war *in your members*?"[39]

How do we subdue "our members" that war against our soul and spirit? Paul gave us the same answer in Romans 6:13 and 6:19: "And do not present *your members* as instruments of unrighteousness to sin, but present yourselves to God as being alive from the dead, and *your members* as instruments of righteousness to God" and "for just as you presented *your members* as slaves of uncleanness, and of lawlessness leading to more lawlessness, so now present *your members* as slaves of righteousness for holiness." Lohse writes, "Depending on

---

[39] See James 4:1.

whom man acknowledges as his Lord, his members are either slaves of 'impurity' and 'iniquity' or obedient servants of 'righteousness.'"[40]

Each day you must present your members to God. Each day we come before Him and surrender all the parts of our body to His grace and glory. We present our hands, feet, eyes, ears, mind, heart, and even our private parts as instruments of righteousness unto God. The Greek word here for "instrument" in Romans 6:13 was an offensive weapon used in war. It is translated as "*armor* of light," "*armor* of righteousness," and "*weapons* of our warfare" in the New Testament. Our members can be used as weapons for good or evil throughout the day. Surrender them to God!

With that understanding of sin and where it works, let's go to the verse for this chapter: Colossians 3:5. It reads, "Therefore put to death your members which are on the earth: fornication, uncleanness, passion, evil desire, and covetousness, which is idolatry." Several translations use the words "sexual immorality, impurity, lust, and evil desires." All of these words can describe sexual sin.

Using a very strong Greek imperative verb of command, Paul says "to put to death your members upon the earth!" Note carefully the wording – "put to death *your members*." Then he describes what that means exactly – "fornication, uncleanness, passion, and evil desires." This is also what Jesus taught when speaking of heart adultery: "If your right eye causes you to sin, pluck it out and cast it from you; for it is more profitable for you that *one of your members* perish, than for your whole body to be cast into hell. And if your right hand causes you to sin, cut it off and cast it from you; for it is more profitable

---

[40] *Colossians and Philemon*, Eduard Lohse, Fortress Press, Philadelphia, Pennsylvania, page 137.

for you that *one of your members* perish, than for your whole body to be cast into hell."[41]

Sexual sin works through your members to disobey God and rebel against His laws.

Exactly how do you put these evil passions to death? In the natural, it's impossible. When it comes to sexual sins, you need supernatural power. That is why Paul wrote in Romans 8:13, "For if you live according to the flesh you will die; but if by the Spirit you put to death the deeds of the body, you will live." Through the Lord's death on the cross, sin was put to death, but it is only by the power of the Spirit that this death becomes a present-day reality. It's "by the Spirit that you put to death the (evil) deeds of the body."

You are not only to "flee fornication"; you also are "to put it to death!" When something is put to death, it has no more life.

If you and your girlfriend have been fornicating in the back seat of your car, you need to put that to death.

If you and your girlfriend have been having sexual intercourse at her apartment, you need to put those encounters to death.

If you and your girlfriend have been going out of town together to hotels to commit sexual sin, it must die today!

If you and your girlfriend are living together and having sex, you must move out and repent of your wickedness.

Again, Lohse says, "In contradistinction to the loose living which was almost universal in the Hellenistic world, Christian teaching demands unconditional obedience to the prohibition on 'fornication.'"[42]

---

[41] See Matthew 5:29-30. See also Matthew 18:8-9 and Mark 9:43, 45, and 47.
[42] See *Colossians and Philemon*, Lohse, page 138.

Barclay writes, "The Christian must kill self-centeredness; he must regard as dead all private desires and ambitions."[43]

Look at the next verse. Colossians 3:6 reads, "Because of these things the wrath of God is coming upon the sons of disobedience." Christians immediately dismiss this verse and say it only applies to unbelievers, but Paul wrote this letter to Christians – "To the saints and faithful brethren in Christ who are in Colosse" (1:2). Christians who fornicate are "sons of disobedience." They are disobedient to the Lord. They provoke the Lord's anger. Fornication is a serious sexual sin with devastating and eternal consequences. It's a work of the flesh that destroys your spiritual life. Never minimize the seriousness of this sin!

Paul goes on to say here in Colossians 3 that we are "to put off the old man with his deeds" and "put on the new man who is renewed in knowledge according to the image of Him who created him." We truly are "God's elect." We are "holy." We are "to put on tender mercies, kindness, humility, meekness, longsuffering, forbearance, forgiveness, and above all, agape love." If you really love your boyfriend, get married. If you are really holy, honor God and repent of your fornication. Put it to death and fear the Lord. Glorify God with your body and your spirit which belong to Him.

It is God's will that you be holy. And one of the main ways to be holy is with your body. Sexual purity delights the heart of God. Let's see what Paul said about that in the next chapter.

YouTube Video: ***Having Sex With Your Boyfriend 09***

---

[43] *The Letters to the Philippians, Colossians, and Thessalonians*, William Barclay, Westminster Press, Philadelphia, Pennsylvania, page 180.

HAVING SEX WITH YOUR BOYFRIEND

10

Don't Fornicate – This is the Will of God

"For this is the will of God, your sanctification: that you should abstain from sexual immorality."

"God's will is for you to be holy, so stay away from all sexual sin." (NLT)
(1 Thessalonians 4:3)

There is no doubt about it – *God commands all Christians everywhere to live a holy life.* Holiness applies to all without exception. It was true in the Old Testament – "You shall therefore be holy, for I am holy" (Leviticus 11:45). It is true in the New Testament – "As He who called you is holy, you also be holy in all your conduct, because it is written, 'Be holy, for I am holy'" (1 Peter 1:15-16).

Here in 1 Thessalonians Chapter 4, Paul reminds believers that "God did not call us to uncleanness (a sexual term), but to holiness" (v7). The Greek word here for "holiness" (hagiasmos) is the same one used in verses 3 and 4 for "your sanctification" and "in

51

sanctification." "Sanctification" means "to make something holy," derived from the Latin word, "sanctus," or "holy." In fact, "hagiasmos" the noun comes from "hagios" in verse 8 when Paul mentions the "*Holy* Spirit." If you reject this call to holiness, you are "rejecting God who has given us His *Holy* Spirit."

The key verse for our discussion is verse 3. "For this is the will of God, your sanctification: that you should abstain from fornication (porneias)." "Abstain" is a verb that means "you hold yourself back from; refrain; keep yourself away from; stay away at a distance." In other words, avoid it at all costs. Run from it. Have nothing to do with fornication. We'll discuss this in Chapter 14.

Let's look quickly at the first eight verses of this chapter and give eight important reasons to avoid sexual immorality.

Abstain from fornication because your Christian walk should please God. In verse 1, Paul said that they had received from Paul the necessary instruction in order "to walk and please God." Purity pleases God. Holiness pleases the Lord. Doing God's will brings Him great delight. Don't fornicate.

Abstain from fornication because this is a command from God. In verse 2, the apostle tells the Thessalonians that "they know what commandments we gave you through the Lord Jesus." "Abstain from fornication" is a commandment given by Jesus as Lord. The Lord Himself is commanding us not to fornicate. He must be obeyed!

Abstain from fornication because this is God's will for your life. It is an essential part of your holiness before Him. Verse 3 teaches us that God wills for you to be sexually pure. When you hold back from fornicating with your boyfriend, you are on the road of holiness.

I remember a Christian man who told me that he drove over to his girlfriend's apartment because he thought she would be there alone. He went there to have sex with her.

He said that he uttered this prayer before God as he drove over: "Lord, if it is not your will for me to have sex with my girlfriend, please stop it. I pray that she won't be home or that she won't open the door. If she is home, I'll assume it's okay to have sex with her."

This is a ridiculous prayer! This is to tempt God. This is a serious violation of God's ways.

No! *You yourself abstain from fornication. This is God's will. It is already revealed. No further discussion is needed.*

Abstain from fornication because as Christians, we want to acquire a wife God's way, not our way. "To possess his own vessel" is a very difficult phrase to interpret here in verse 4, and many godly scholars have disagreed over its true meaning. Some say "vessel" means "a man's physical body" like 2 Corinthians 4:7; others say it means your "wife" (1 Peter 3:7) or how you "acquire your wife." I interpret it to mean how a man acquires his wife. Do we receive a wife from the Lord "in sanctification and honor" or do we get one "in passion of lust, like the Gentiles who do not know God" (v5)?

When you are having sex with your girlfriend, you are living in darkness. You are out of God's will. You are not walking in holiness; you are corrupting and defiling yourself. How can you discern God's will? I've known so many Christian singles who began having sexual intercourse with their boyfriends and girlfriends (some have even gotten pregnant), and they are confused about whether to get married or not.

Keep yourself pure. Do it God's way. Abstain from sexual sin. Seek God's will above everything else. When you are keeping yourself pure, you will "see God" and see His will for your life.

Honor your future wife by keeping yourself pure.

53

Abstain from fornication so that you don't act and live like unbelievers (pagans, Gentiles) who don't know God. To fornicate is to live in lust. To fornicate is to live in unholy passion. You are giving in to the works of the flesh. People who don't know God do this. This is not so for the Christian believer. We keep ourselves pure. We wait until our wedding night. We abstain until we're married. This is not a prudish way; this is God's way.

I love that short sentence right in the middle of the Sermon on the Mount. It says simply, "Therefore do not be like them."[44] Don't be like unbelievers. Don't act like they act.

I read briefly a biography of a well-known Hollywood actress. The article said that she started living with her first boyfriend but never married him. Then she started living with another boyfriend and married him for a few years. She divorced him, and while going through divorce proceedings, she moved in with her new boyfriend. She married him, then divorced two years later. She quickly found a new boyfriend, moved in, and got married one year later. She then divorced him, and even before the divorce was final, she was already on a cruise with her new boyfriend. She left him, and started a relationship with another man.

This is "the passion of lust of Gentiles who do not know God" (v5). Don't be like them. Know God's will and walk in it.

Abstain from fornication because it will open a door to further sexual sin even after you are married. I've learned that most fornicators become adulterers. Sadly, this is true even among Christians. So many believers I know had sexual intercourse prior to marrying their current wife/husband, and later on I find them having sex with someone else's spouse! They are out of control.

---

[44] See Matthew 6:8.

Verse 6 is pretty scary: "That no one should take advantage of and defraud his brother in this matter, because the Lord is the avenger of all such, as we also forewarned you and testified." Ironman, Hulk, Captain America, and Thor are avengers, but God also is an avenger! Paul wrote, "'Vengeance is Mine, I will repay,' says the Lord," and the author of Hebrews said, "For we know Him who said, 'Vengeance is Mine, I will repay,' says the Lord." He concludes by saying, "It is a fearful thing to fall into the hands of the living God."[45]

I sat down once with a Christian man who was devastated by his adultery with another man's wife. When I asked him to give me some history of his present relationship with his own wife, he explained that he fornicated a lot with his wife before they got married. He didn't "acquire his wife in sanctification and honor," and now he was messing with someone else's wife in an unholy and dishonorable way. He fornicated with his girlfriend, and now he's committing adultery with another man's wife! He was out of control before marriage and now he's out of control within marriage! So often, fornicators turn into adulterers. Don't do this.

Abstain from fornication because God did not call us to uncleanness, but to holiness. If you are a Christian, and you are having sex with your boyfriend, you feel dirty spiritually. You are unclean. You are defiled. You feel guilty and condemned. Your conscience is greatly troubled. Your body was not made for sexual immorality; it was made for the Lord.

A young Christian man came to see me after one of our Sunday services. He was totally depressed. He had difficulty telling me what was happening with him. Tears welled up in his eyes. He could hardly speak. He walked away with his head down. I didn't hear about him for

---

[45] See Romans 12:19; Hebrews 10:30-31.

nearly a year. His Christian parents later told me that he had gotten his girlfriend pregnant. Don't live this way. There is a better way.

Abstain from fornication because if you don't, you are rejecting God who gave you His holy commandment and His Holy Spirit. The Greek word here for "reject" in verse 8 is often translated "despised" in other verses. It has the idea of disrespecting the Lord. You don't really fear what He commands. You're choosing to do things your way. Without saying it, you're telling the Lord, "I know this is wrong; I know you command me not to do it, but I'm going to do it anyway. I'm free. I'm lonely. I have needs. I'm going to have sex with my girlfriend. I'm going to ignore what you say and do what pleases me." This is a very dangerous way of thinking. Williams writes, "Whoever regards sexual sin as a matter of little consequence is guilty of discounting God."[46]

Abstain from fornication!

Our entire culture and society are corrupted by sexual sins. Our governments, schools, universities, businesses, sports, social media, and churches are overwhelmed and dominated by fornication. Let's see why in the next chapter.

YouTube Video: **Having Sex With Your Boyfriend 10**

---

[46] *1 and 2 Thessalonians*, David J. Williams, New International Biblical Commentary, Hendrickson Publishers, Peabody, Massachusetts, page 75.

11

A Culture Corrupted by Fornication

*"God has judged the great harlot who
corrupted the earth with her fornication."*

*"He has punished the prostitute who made
the earth evil with her sexual sin." (NCV)*

*"Our God has punished the prostitute. She
is the one who ruined the earth with her
sexual sin." (ERV)
(Revelation 19:2)*

I stand amazed at the incredible images and visions that the apostle John saw in the book of Revelation. They are dramatic, startling, and powerful. We are at once astonished, shocked, and unsettled.

John doesn't see the devil; he sees a dragon with seven heads and ten horns. He doesn't see Jesus; he sees a Lamb as though slain with seven horns and seven eyes. He doesn't see demons; he sees locusts that look like horses with scorpion tails, women's hair, and men's faces.

He sees creatures that are full of eyes with six wings and the faces of a lion, a calf, a man and a flying eagle. John sees white, red, black, and pale horses racing across a cosmic landscape causing death and destruction. He sees a beast with seven heads and ten horns and a body of a leopard, feet of a bear, and the mouth of a lion. He sees vultures, eagles, and angels flying around. The apostle sees and has a personal encounter with a giant angel clothed with a cloud, a rainbow on his head, a face like the sun, and feet like pillars of fire.

He sees an amazing heavenly vision of Jesus, highly exalted and radiant, with eyes of flaming fire, hair and head as white as snow, feet like fine brass, and a mouth with a sharp two-edged sword. Later, John sees the Lord riding on a white horse while crowned with many crowns bringing judgment on the nations and destroying enemy armies and beasts. What he sees causes him "to fall at His feet as dead" (1:17).

One of the most profound images he sees is a "great prostitute" who is corrupting "the kings of the earth" and "the inhabitants of the world" with "her fornication." Her influence is so far-reaching that she has everyone "drunk with the wine of her fornication." She herself is drunk "with the blood of saints and with the blood of the martyrs of Jesus." So astonishing is this sight that John writes, "When I saw her, I marveled with great amazement" (17:7).

He notices something on her head. He says in Revelation 17:5: "On her forehead a name was written: MYSTERY, BABYLON THE GREAT, THE MOTHER OF HARLOTS AND OF THE ABOMINATIONS OF THE EARTH." She is the source; she gives birth to every prostitute and abominable thing on planet earth.

Nearly twenty times in Revelation alone, John uses the words "pornos," "pornē," "porneia," or "porneuō." John sees fornicators living in fornication.

Not only does John see it in the world, he hears Jesus expose it in the church (2:14, 2:20, 2:21). Sadly, he also sees fornicators burning forever in the lake of fire!

The great prostitute has a worldwide influence in Revelation. *She corrupts the whole world with sexual immorality*.

Consider these verses: "She made all nations drink of the wine of the wrath of her fornication" (14:8), "with whom the kings of the earth have committed fornication, and the inhabitants of the earth have been made drunk with the wine of her fornication" (17:2), "she has a golden cup in her hand full of abominations and filthiness of her fornication" (17:4), "all nations have drunk of the wine of the wrath of her fornication, and the kings of the earth have committed fornication with her" (18:3), "the great whore, which did corrupt the earth with her fornication" (19:2), and "the kings of the earth, who have committed fornication and lived deliciously with her" (18:9). The kings of the earth and the inhabitants of the world are fornicating with her. Her fornication brings "the wrath" of God.

Why did the Lord choose to illustrate the world and all that it represents with a prostitute? Why not use a drunk, a thief, a murderer, or a witch? Why use an image of a woman who sells her body for sex? She literally has the whole world "intoxicated" with her sexual wine. She has gotten into everyone's veins.

I believe the most devastating sins in our society are sexual sins. Who can calculate the wreckage of human lives associated with molestation, rape, pornography, adultery, fornication, homosexuality, prostitution, bestiality, transgenderism, teen pregnancies, and human trafficking?

And our governments, schools, and universities send mixed messages that only create confusion. They decry child pornography but support homosexuality; they oppose human trafficking but accept fornication; they fight against rape but embrace transgenderism. The sports world is full of sexual immorality. Many of the most famous athletes in the world are living with their girlfriends. A large parentage of the best women players in the Women's National Basketball Association (WNBA) are lesbians (Diana Taurasi, Brittney Griner, Sue Bird, Breanna Stewart, Elena Donne, Candace Parker). Dr. Larry Nassar, the team doctor of the USA women's gymnastics program, sexually abused hundreds of young women. All of these examples can be defined as fornication.

The great prostitute is sitting on many waters suffocating the life out of millions of people. She floods the airwaves of television, radio, movies, and the Internet with her filthy sexual perversions. Counseling centers are filled with the ruined lives of men, women, and children who are overwhelmed by the out of control sexual behavior of family members.

Recently, in one year, the National Center for Missing and Exploited Children (NCMEC) processed 29.3 million reports of sexual abuse material including videos and images. They now handle up to 80,000 daily reports, many of these reports are filed by tech companies like FaceBook, Twitter, and Snapchat. The prostitute is an influencer everywhere.

The Bible is full of stories of sexual immorality. Sodom and Gomorrah were overrun by homosexuality. The Canaanites were "vomited out of the land" by sexual perversions. David committed adultery against Bathsheba and killed her husband. Shechem raped Dinah. Amon sexually violated his sister Tamar. The Levite's concubine was gang raped. Paul handed a Christian man over to Satan for having sex with his father's wife. 24,000 Israelites were killed in one day for fornicating with

Moabite women. Ruben had sex with his father Jacob's wife. There are too many disastrous stories to tell.

Closer to home, in our church, we have a man that was molested repeatedly by his older brother and another man who was seduced by a nun! Several women were molested by their father…for years. One lady was raped by her boyfriend. Two men were molested by older neighborhood kids. Another woman was sexually abused by her step-father. Teenagers have gotten pregnant by their boyfriends. Both men and women have committed adultery. Some have struggled daily with pornography.

You might ask, "Why mention all this ugly stuff? Can't you talk about something more positive?"

I wrote this chapter to say one thing to all of us. *Utterly and totally reject the Babylonian prostitute and her fornication! Get out of Babylon! If you're living with your boyfriend, move out. Sexual immorality is corrupting your life. Repent of fornication.*

Revelation 18:4-6 reveals God's judgment and warning against the great whore: "And I heard another voice from heaven saying, 'Come out of her, my people, lest you share in her sins, and lest you receive of her plagues. For her sins have reached to heaven, and God has remembered her iniquities. Render to her just as she rendered to you, and repay her double according to her works; in the cup which she has mixed, mix double for her." Fornication is not a pleasurable sin. It is a great curse that will destroy your life. It incurs the judgment of God. Get out of it. Return to Jesus. Reject the wine of the Babylonian prostitute.

One of the churches in Revelation was overrun by fornication. Let's look at this church next and see what Jesus told these 1st Century Christians.

YouTube Video: **Having Sex With Your Boyfriend 11**

HAVING SEX WITH YOUR BOYFRIEND

12

Giving You Space to Repent of Fornication

"And I gave her time to repent of her sexual immorality, and she did not repent."
(Revelation 2:21)

It is a terrible reality, but fornication is in the church of the living God. Christians of all ages and from different backgrounds are engaging in sexual immorality. The apostle Paul dealt extensively with sexual immorality in churches at Rome, Corinth, Galatia, Ephesus, Colosse, and Thessalonica. Jesus exposed the sexual sins in the churches of Pergamos and Thyatira. To this day, nearly 2,000 years later, churches are still battling sexual darkness among its members.

In just the last few years, I've talked to Pastors and Christian leaders who have been devastated by the corrupt actions of pastors, elders, worship leaders and singers, youth pastors, teenagers, Sunday School teachers, evangelism directors, and administrators who are indulging in pornography, having sexual intercourse with boyfriends/girlfriends, or living in homosexual or lesbian relationships. It is a veritable flood of ungodliness that is corrupting our young people. And rest assured – as we will learn in this chapter – the judgments of the Lord will come upon such behavior. Churches and their pastors are shaken to the core by such sins and judgments. These things are antithetical to who we should be as God's people. As Paul wrote, "Let everyone who names the name of Christ depart from iniquity" or "all who belong to the Lord must turn away from evil."[47]

In Revelation 2:12-17, the exalted Lord Jesus spoke to the church at Pergamos. The section title in my Bible for these verses is "The Compromising Church." These believers had allowed "the doctrine of Balaam" to enter, and now they were living in idolatry and "committing sexual immorality." In Numbers Chapter 25, Balaam had taught King Balak to corrupt the Israelites by bringing in Moabite women for sex. Incredibly, 24,000 of God's people died in one day because of sexual sin.

In Revelation 2:18-29, Jesus also spoke to the church at Thyatira. The section title in my Bible for these verses is "The Corrupt Church." This time, it was not Balaam, but "Jezebel" who deceived the church. Verse 20 reads, "You allow that woman Jezebel, who calls herself a prophetess, to teach and seduce My servants to commit sexual immorality and eat things sacrificed to idols." Different teacher/doctrine, but the same results.

Whoever is allowed to teach in a local church begins to have tremendous influence. When Jezebel started teaching, sexual immorality was the fruit. Note the words "porneuō" (v20), "porneuō" (v21), and "adultery" (v22) in three consecutive verses. With Jezebel, sexual sins flourish.

---

[47] See 2 Timothy 2:19.

Revelation 2:21 is very insightful: "I gave her time to repent of her sexual immorality, and she did not repent." One translation correctly renders the last phrase as "but she is *unwilling*" (Greek, "ou thelei"). Jesus had given Jezebel time to repent, but she was unwilling. She refused. "This suggests that the present letter is not the first time Christ has tried to deal with her,"[48] and indicates she knew of Christ's judgment, but she ignored it and continued in her evil ways.

I remember a young Christian lady in our church who was involved in several areas of ministry. She was on fire for the Lord. Suddenly, in a moment of loneliness and compromise, she started dating an unbeliever without letting anyone in her family or our church know. After a few weeks, they were having sex. It was not long afterward that she moved in with him and left our church. When I went to her apartment to confront her (and him), she said I was "judging her" and asked me to leave. She was "unwilling" to repent. Several years later, she was still living with her boyfriend.

So many of us are stubborn. We don't want to change. We are comfortable living in our sin and compromise. Some of the most devastating judgments in the Bible are found in the trumpet judgments of Revelation Chapters 8-9; and yet, even after such fearful events, we read in Revelation 9:21 – "And they did not repent of their murders or their sorceries or their *sexual immorality* or their thefts." Jesus says, "Stop!"; the people say, "No!" There is a defiance here that is frightening.

Sexual immorality always brings punishment *and sickness*. The next verse, verse 22, says, "Indeed I will cast her into a sickbed, and those who commit adultery with her into great tribulation, unless they repent of their

---

[48] *Revelation*, Gordon D. Fee, New Covenant Commentary Series, Cascade Books, Eugene, Oregon, page 40.

deeds." One translation reads, "I am going to strike down Jezebel. Everyone who does these immoral things with her will also be punished, if they don't stop." Someone has translated it as – "I will throw both her and those who sleep with her onto a sleeping mat where they will suffer terribly."[49]

Jesus will throw her, not into a bed for sleep (or sex), but into a bed for sickness. There are beds for homes, and there are beds for hospitals. As Kepler writes, "A bed of illness will soon replace the bed of adultery for the woman and her devotees."[50] She thought she was giving love, but it only resulted in sickness. The "bed of sin" has become the "bed of pain."

The words, "committing adultery," are a Greek present tense participial verb or "they keep on committing adultery with her." As stated before, they refuse to stop. They are unwilling. They continue in their rebellious ways. Nevertheless, Jesus commanded "Jezebel" to repent (v21) and now also all of her followers ("those," "they") (v22).

Prophecy students are worried about "the Great Tribulation" (v22) at the end of the age. I think more believers should be concerned about "adultery" which also brings "great tribulation" (NKJV) or "a bed of suffering" (NIV).

Verse 23 is a very severe verse! It is not difficult to understand; it's just difficult to accept...but Jesus is walking among His churches and dealing with our sins! It says, "I will kill her children with death, and all the churches shall know that I am He who searches the minds and hearts. And I will give to each one of you according

---

[49] See the United Bible Society (UBS) translation notes for this verse.
[50] *The Book of Revelation*, Thomas S. Kepler, Oxford University Press, New York, New York, page 63.

to your works." Jesus wants "ALL the churches" to know how serious He is!

"Search" is a Greek present tense participle that means Jesus "keeps on searching." This church must remember that "these things says the Son of God, who has eyes like a flame of fire" (2:18). Jezebel may have deceived the church, but she does not fool the exalted Son of God!

The main sex organ in a person is his brain. Fornication and adultery always start in the mind (thoughts) and heart. And this is where His flaming eyes are looking – your mind. Jesus said in Mark 7:20-23, "What comes out of a man, that defiles a man. For from within, out of the heart of men, *proceed evil thoughts, adulteries, fornications*…all these evil things come from within and defile a man." Evil thoughts come from the heart. Jesus is looking at everything we're thinking.

Thank God that Jesus always gives us room (space) to repent. If He brought judgment right away on any and all sins, none of us would survive.

If you are having sex with anyone right now that you're not married to, you need to repent. In His mercy, God is giving you time to repent and get restored to a right relationship with Him.

In the next chapter, we will examine one of the most consequential verses on fornication in the entire Bible. Let's go to 1 Corinthians 10 and see what Paul said happened to Israel in the wilderness. His people were destroyed because of fornication.

YouTube Video: **Having Sex With Your Boyfriend 12**

HAVING SEX WITH YOUR BOYFRIEND

13

Fornication Destroys Lives

"We should not commit sexual immorality,
as some of them did – and in one day
twenty-three thousand of them died."
(1 Corinthians 10:8)

The "Wilderness Generation" was that group of Israelites who were supernaturally delivered from Egyptian bondage by the strong arm of the Lord, but were then completely defeated and destroyed in the wilderness because of their disobedience and rebellion. Out of 603,550 men of military age, only two – Joshua and Caleb – made it into the Promised Land!

In 1 Corinthians 10:6-10, the apostle Paul lists five sins that kept God's people out of the Promised Land: 1) Lust, 2) idolatry, 3) sexual immorality, 4) tempting the Lord, and 5) complaining. *And these are the same five sins that keep Christian believers in bondage today.* For our discussion in this chapter, let's focus on verse 8. This is one of the most devastating verses on fornication in the entire Bible. There were 23,000 funerals in one day!

Make careful note of this wording: "Nor let us commit sexual immorality, as some of them did, and in one day twenty-three thousand died."

It's interesting that in the Greek text, "porneuō," is mentioned twice – with the words "commit" and "sexual immorality." Literally in Greek, it reads, "Neither let us fornicate as some of them fornicated."

The only thing Paul tells us about this fornication is how God judged it. 23,000 of God's people died in a single day! This is one of the greatest judgments against Israel in the entire Old Testament. This judgment is part of verse 6 above – "God was not pleased with most of them; their bodies were scattered in the wilderness." 23,000 dead bodies on the desert floor – all because of sexual sin!

And remember what Paul said before and after these five sins. They are "examples" to us. Paul was warning the Corinthians then and he is warning Christians now. Verse 6 begins, "Now these things became our examples." Verse 11 also begins, "Now all these things happened to them as examples." He adds, "And they were written down as warnings to us who live at the end of the age." Paul is not merely giving us interesting historical information; he is warning the Corinthian believers that the same thing could happen to them. In fact, he warns them further with verse 12: "Therefore let him who thinks he stands take heed lest he fall." Don't think it can't happen to you!

I don't want to admit this, but many years ago, our local church was rocked by scandalous sexual escapades. One of our church elders ran off with the worship leader's wife; another church leader was secretly in bondage to Internet pornography and he was going to San Francisco on weekends to watch live sex acts; one of our ushers was having sex with a recently divorced woman who was seducing him after Sunday services. We claimed to be a "Spirit-filled church" that was dedicated to following Jesus Christ as Lord. I was not without sin and I could never cast the first stone, but my heart was grieved, and my wife and I wanted to leave the church. I cannot adequately describe everything that was going on in the church, but one thing I did discern: *We were under God's judgment!* The words of Jesus to the Ephesian church in Revelation 2:5 kept running through my mind: "Repent or else I will come to you quickly and remove your lampstand from its place – unless you repent." It is a miracle of God's mercy and grace that we survived as a church, all because of several leaders' careless disregard of God's laws.

We thought we were standing, but we fell. I remembered that verse from Proverbs: "Pride goes before destruction, and a haughty spirit before a fall."[51]

What Old Testament story was Paul referring to in 1 Corinthians 10:8? It was the disastrous encounter that the Israelites had with the Moabite women in Numbers 25. Balaam could not curse Israel from the outside, so he taught Balak how to curse them from the inside. Numbers 31:16 reads, "Look, these women caused the children of Israel, through the counsel of Balaam, to trespass against the Lord in the incident of Peor, and there was a plague among the congregation of the Lord."

These women not only brought their bodies; they brought their gods. Idolatry and sexual immorality always go together. When Jesus spoke of Balaam, He said that he "taught Balak to put a stumbling block before the children of Israel, to eat things sacrificed to idols, and to commit sexual immorality."[52] Numbers 25:2 says, "They invited the people to the sacrifices of their gods, and the people ate and bowed down to their gods." The

---

[51] See Proverbs 16:18.
[52] See Revelation 2:14. Jezebel did the same thing (2:20).

next verse says they actually "joined themselves to the worship of Baal of Peor" (v3). Before they gave themselves to sexual immorality, they gave themselves to idolatrous worship.

God's very people – whom He delivered from Egyptian bondage – were so emboldened to sexual sin that one of the leaders of the tribe of Simeon named Zimri took "a Midianite woman" and started having sex with her in his tent "before the sight of Moses and the sight of all the congregation of Israel."

Phinehas the priest, Aaron's grandson, was so enraged in the fear of God that he took a large javelin in his hand and ran to that same tent. While in the very act of fornicating, Phinehas thrust the spear through both the man and the woman. By God's power, that single act of zeal ("he was zealous for My zeal" and "he was zealous for his God") "stopped the plague among the children of Israel" (v8).

I have a simple message for you from Moses in Numbers 25 and Paul in 1 Corinthians 10 – *Fornication will destroy your life*. Yes, you may enjoy a few moments of pleasure with your girlfriend, but you are plaguing yourself with unseen curses that will bring you down. When you fornicate, you are playing with fire and you will be burned! When speaking of sexual sin, Solomon asks, "Can a man take fire to his bosom, and his clothes not be burned? Can one walk on hot coals, and his feet not be seared?"[53] Repent right now of your sexual sin; otherwise, God will judge you as Hebrews 13:4 reveals.

In the next chapter, let's talk about your body as God's temple.

YouTube Video: **Having Sex With Your Boyfriend 13**

---

[53] See Proverbs 6:27-28.

14

Abstain from Fornication

*"For it seemed good to the Holy Spirit, and
to us, to lay upon you no greater burden
than these necessary things: that you abstain
from things offered to idols, from blood,
from things strangled, and from sexual
immorality. If you keep yourselves from
these, you will do well."*
(Acts 15:28-29)

Government and university studies in the United States and United Kingdom both confirm that 75% of people aged 18 through 29 believe that it is acceptable for unmarried couples to live together even if they don't plan to marry. The numbers are startling, but people who are cohabiting now outnumber those wanting to get married and those who want to stay single. More and more people are not dating and remaining in their apartments or houses; they are simply moving in together out of convenience, economic benefit, and also because there are not as many stigmas against cohabitation as with previous generations.

Simply put, people today start dating, move in, begin fornicating, and really have no plans to get married.

Let's enjoy the benefits of married life without getting married, they believe. "Galena Rhoades, research professor in psychology and director of the Family Research Center at the University of Denver, agrees that changing social attitudes around cohabiting have enabled younger generations to adopt a more casual attitude around moving in together, rather than viewing it as a test-run for marriage. 'Cohabiting is becoming more and more a stage in dating, rather than a stage in marriage,' says Rhoades."[54]

They call it "bunking up," "shacking up," "moving in," and "cohabitation." No one calls it "fornication."

They call themselves "couples," "partners," "cohabitants," and "romantic partners." No one calls themselves "fornicators."

And no one calls it sexual sin. No one says it is sexual immorality. Of course, today's dark culture is ignorant of God's laws and standards. Our society's beliefs about marriage and sex have degraded so much that pretty much anything is acceptable. Unfortunately, these beliefs have been embraced by many Christians in our churches.

Today, Christians who speak out against sexual immorality – sex between boyfriends and girlfriends – are viewed as judgmental, prudish, legalistic, and pharisaical. They are accused of being narrow-minded, bigots, haters, and not progressive enough for today's agendas.

Despite what people might say to me after seeing or reading this book, I want to be a voice in the wilderness calling everyone to repentance and faith in the Lord. Fornication destroys lives. Sexual sin sends people to an eternal hell. Having sex with your boyfriend defiles and

---

[54] See the British Broadcasting Company's (BBC) article, *Why Millennials aren't moving in together as a trial marriage*, dated April 8, 2022.

corrupts people. Sexual immorality undermines the marriage institution like no other sin.

This book is a call to abstinence. The Lord commands us "to abstain." Paul wrote, "For this is the will of God, even your sanctification: that you *abstain* from sexual immorality (porneia)." Peter said, "Beloved, I beg you as sojourners and pilgrims, *abstain* from fleshly lusts which war against the soul." Another verse reads, "*Abstain* from every appearance of evil."[55]

"Abstain" and "abstinence" come from the same Latin word. They mean "to hold yourself away; to refrain." The New Testament Greek word (apechomai) is very similar in definition: "To hold oneself off; to keep oneself away; to keep your distance." Don't do it. Stay away. Flee fornication.

It's interesting to me that in the book of Acts, the word "fornication" appears only three times, and each time it comes with the admonition "to abstain from sexual immorality." The apostle James told the council at Jerusalem in Acts 15:19-20, "Therefore I judge that we should not trouble those from among the Gentiles who are turning to God, but that we write to them *to abstain* from things polluted by idols, *from sexual immorality* (porneia), from things strangled, and from blood." In Acts 15:28-29, they sent a letter to all the Gentiles in Antioch, Syria, and Cilicia saying, "For it seemed good to the Holy Spirit, and to us, to lay upon you no greater burden than these necessary things: that you *abstain* from things offered to idols, from blood, from things strangled, and *from sexual immorality* (porneia). If you *keep yourselves from these*, you will do well. Farewell." Acts 21:25 reads, "But concerning the Gentiles who believe, we have written and decided that they should observe no such thing, except that they *should keep*

---

[55] See 1 Thessalonians 4:3; 1 Peter 2:11; 1 Thessalonians 5:22.

themselves from things offered to idols, from blood, from things strangled, and *from sexual immorality* (porneia)."

While being told to avoid pagan practices regarding idols and the eating of blood with meats, the only moral requirement was "to abstain from sexual immorality." It was so prevalent and widespread that the apostles felt it was critical that they highlight the danger of this sin.

Did you see the wording? "This seemed good to the Holy Spirit," "these are necessary things," "if you keep yourselves from these things," "abstain from sexual immorality," and "that they should keep themselves from sexual immorality." The apostles could have listed other sins like those prohibited in the Ten Commandments (killing, stealing, coveting, or bearing false witness). They didn't want "to lay upon you any greater burden." Fornication was the dominant sin back then, and it has quickly become the most rampant now.

As Christians, we abstain. As believers in Christ, we practice abstinence. As disciples of Jesus, we hold ourselves back. This is not legalism; this is holiness.

We can obey the Lord because of the cross of Christ – "We died to sin; how can we live in it any longer?" We can obey the Lord because of the Holy Spirit – "The fruit of the Spirit is patience and self-control." We can obey the Lord because of prayer – "Do not lead us into temptation, but deliver us from the evil one."[56]

Let us embrace this truth: "If you keep yourselves from these – including fornication – you will do well."

In the next chapter, let's see how fornication affects your physical body and the body of Christ.

YouTube Video: **Having Sex With Your Boyfriend 14**

---

[56] See Romans 6:2; Galatians 5:22-23; Matthew 6:13.

15

Fornication and Your Body

*"Do you not know that your bodies are
members of Christ? Shall I then take the
members of Christ and make them members
of a harlot? Certainly not! Or do you not
know that he who is joined to a harlot is one
body with her? For 'the two,' He says,
'shall become one flesh.'"*
(1 Corinthians 6:15-16)

Paul mentions the word "body" or "bodies" nearly fifty times in 1 Corinthians. He talked about so many different bodies, both physical and spiritual. Paul taught that "the believer's body is not for sexual immorality but for the Lord" (6:13); the Christian's physical body is "the temple of the Holy Spirit" and we must "glorify God in our body" (6:19-20); "husbands and wives have authority over the other's body" (7:3-4); single Christian women must "be holy in both body and spirit" before the Lord (7:34); his own physical body had "to be disciplined" and "brought into subjection" so that he would not be "disqualified" in his preaching ministry (9:27); "the bodies" of the Israelites "were scattered in the wilderness" because of their disobedience (10:5); the physical body of the Lord – "this is My body which was broken for you, do this in remembrance of Me" (11:24); Christians "form one body with many members" (12:12, 12:20); "wheat and other grains" have been "given a body as God pleases, and to each seed its own body" (15:38); there are "celestial bodies" and "terrestrial bodies" like "the sun, moon, and stars" (15:40); and at the final resurrection, "our natural body" will be given "a spiritual body" (15:44).

Paul makes the startling claim that our physical bodies are actually "members of Christ" (6:15). Our limbs are the limbs of Christ. By the sovereign grace of God, we are so united with Christ that upon receiving Him as Lord and Savior, we become one with Him. He writes, "He who is joined to the Lord becomes one spirit with Him" (6:17). He asks the rhetorical question in 6:15: "Shall I then take the members of Christ (our physical bodies) and make them (join them as) members of a harlot (pornēs, literally a female fornicator)?" His immediate answer is "certainly not!" "No way!" "Absolutely not!" This is going to corrupt and infect the whole body like we will discuss in the next chapter. A little yeast is going to get into the whole batch of dough.

Morris writes, "It is this that makes sexual vice so abhorrent. The horrible thing about this sin is that 'the members of Christ' are taken away from their proper use (the service of Christ) and made 'members of a prostitute.' There is a horrible profanation of that which should be used only for Christ."[57]

Paul asks a third question in verse 16: "Or do you not know that he who is joined to a harlot (fornicator) is one body with her?" He describes sexual intercourse as one "who is joined." This Greek present tense participle indicates literally that you are "continually being glued"

---

[57] See *1 Corinthians*, Leon Morris, page 97.

to the girl you're having sex with. The verb means that you will "stick together." You will become so connected to the fornicator that Paul quotes from Genesis 2:24 and says, "For 'the two,' He says, 'shall become one flesh.'" Rather than join yourself to the Lord in your spirit, you are joined to the fornicator in your body. This verse from Genesis was for "a man who shall be joined to his wife," not for boyfriends and girlfriends.

Over the years, I have seen so many Christian singles – both males and females – struggle terribly to break off relationships that are destroying and poisoning their lives. They just can't seem to get away. They go back again and again to relationships because they are "glued together." Once they start having sex, they "became one" and they can't seem to separate. It seems like spirit, soul, and body have become one because of fornication and they can't break free. "There is a profound psycho-physical union in sexual consummation. Sexual relations forge a profound relationship between two people."[58]

Sexual intercourse is a powerful physical act given by God for married couples to keep them "glued together." The flesh, the world, and the devil have defiled this beautiful act that God intended for good, and it has been turned into something that brings people into bondage. So many young men who are coming to Christ have defiled and glued themselves to so many women that they are filled with sexual confusion and darkness. They live from one fantasy to another in their minds of previous sexual encounters with ex-girlfriends. These "soul-ties" go into marriages and cause great confusion.

Also, I agree with David Prior who writes that "this is the strongest reason why believers ought not to marry unbelievers. Simply because there is no true

---

[58] See *1 Corinthians*, Thomas Schreiner, page 128.

oneness and therefore there should be no one-flesh either."[59]

Can you imagine all the confusion Solomon had in his life? In 1 Kings 11:3, we learn that he had at least one thousand women! "And he had seven hundred wives, princesses, and three hundred concubines; and his wives turned away his heart." No wonder his heart became so dark and idolatrous. His heart was scattered and shattered by all his sexual escapades.

What is Paul's answer to all of the fornication and sexual confusion? *He says that your body doesn't belong to you; it belongs to the Lord.* A few verses later, Paul says, "Or do you not know that your body is the temple of the Holy Spirit who is in you, whom you have from God, and you are not your own? For you were bought at a price; therefore, glorify God in your body and in your spirit, which are God's."[60] Christians can't do whatever they want with their bodies. Their bodies belong to God. He is the owner. He possesses the body. He lives in our body by the Holy Spirit. We are the holy temple where God's Spirit dwells.

And Paul had written a few verses earlier, "The body is not for sexual immorality but for the Lord, and the Lord for the body" (6:13). Your body doesn't belong to your boyfriend; it belongs to the Lord. You are God's property. You are God's possession. He truly owns you. Again, you can't do whatever you want with your physical body.

In the next chapter, let's see how fornication brings disastrous infections into the church body.

YouTube Video: **Having Sex With Your Boyfriend 15**

---

[59] *The Message of 1 Corinthians*, David Prior, The Bible Speaks Today, Inter-Varsity Press, Downers Grove, Illinois, page 102.
[60] 1 Corinthians 6:19-20.

16

Fornication Infects the Church of God

*"I wrote to you in my epistle not to keep
company with fornicators."*
(1 Corinthians 5:9)

In December of 2020, at the height of the COVID-19 pandemic, a Pastor friend of mine went to Los Angeles for a family Christmas gathering. One relative showed up with COVID, and a few days later, about twenty family members had the virus. At the beginning of the COVID pandemic, another pastor had a church fellowship in this backyard where one person came who had the virus, and by the end of the week, nearly thirty-five people were infected.

Viruses spread; so does sinful behavior. When speaking of sexual sin, Paul asks in 1 Corinthians 5:6, "Do you not know that a little leaven leavens the whole lump?" When speaking of legalism, Paul says in Galatians 5:9, "A little leaven leavens the whole lump." In other words, "A little yeast works through the whole batch of dough." This is the subject of this chapter – just like the virus and just like leaven, sexual sin spreads.

The verse we are considering – 1 Corinthians 5:9 – appears right after Paul's teaching on "leaven." It reads, "I wrote to you in my epistle not to keep company with fornicators." The very long Greek word translated "to keep company with" (sunanmignusthai) means literally "to mix yourself up with." Some translations say "do not associate with" or "have nothing to do with" fornicators. Verse 11 below adds, "I have written to you not to keep company with anyone named a brother, who is sexually immoral...not even to eat with such a person." If a man said he was a Christian but was living with his girlfriend, you were not allowed to even have lunch with him. You rejected any type of fellowship. Fee comments, "They are to disassociate from a brother who lives as though he were still in the world."[61]

Paul concludes in verse 12-13, God judges outsiders (unbelievers), but Christians were to judge insiders (believers). Quoting a verse from Deuteronomy, Paul commands, "Put away from yourselves the evil person." The apostle had no hesitation calling such a professed believer "an evil person." He was evil. He would infect the church with his evil behavior. In the next chapter, Paul will say that fornicators are part of "the unrighteous" who "will not inherit the kingdom of God" (6:9-10). Fornicators go to hell.

This is an extremely unpopular position with many of today's comprising churches in the United States and other Western countries. I recently officiated a funeral at a church facility of a Lutheran church that not only welcomed homosexuals, lesbians, transgenders, and fornicators, but also "celebrated" their perversions. There was no separation from the world's behaviors and lifestyles. They openly accept, embrace, and fellowship with the sexually immoral people of our corrupt culture.

---

[61] See *The First Epistle to the Corinthians*, Gordon Fee, page 221.

On the contrary, the apostle Paul handed one man over to Satan for sexual sin. He told us to refuse any fellowship with those living immoral lives.

If you are a Christian believer, and you are having sex with your girlfriend, viewing pornography on the Internet, or watching R/X-rated movies, you are infected. If you do not repent, other Christians must stop fellowshipping with you. Christians should not invite you over to their house nor eat any meal with you. You should be put out of the church. This is necessary for the sanctity and purity of the church. Your "little leaven" can infect the whole batch of Christians. This is "the old leaven" of "malice and wickedness" (v8). It is a sin that will infiltrate the church and corrupt it.

That's what the apostle Paul did. He not only put a man out of fellowship with the church, he actually "delivered (handed) him over to Satan for the destruction of the flesh, that his spirit may be saved in the day of the Lord Jesus."[62] The Corinthians were "glorying" and "puffed up" that a man was having sex with his father's wife! Paul said they should rather have "mourned" or "grieved" (v2) this sexual sin that not even the pagan unbelievers were doing. J. B. Phillips translated it as "an immorality of a kind that even pagans condemn." Wow, what a verdict against the Corinthian church![63]

Several years ago, we began reaching out to a man who was married and had four small children. He was struggling in his marriage. After a few counseling sessions, he gave up on his marriage and moved in with another woman (who had recently gone through a divorce). I found out that this man and his new girlfriend started attending another church here in our city. I called

---

[62] See 1 Corinthians 5:5.
[63] Commentator David Prior, a South African, called 1 & 2 Corinthians, 1 & 2 Californians because of the prevalence of sexual sins in this state. What a terrible comparison!

that church and explained that there was a man now attending there that was committing adultery with another woman and had abandoned his family. The assistant pastor who took my call said that they don't judge people. They accept them and hope that over time they will change and follow the Lord.

Christians can leave one church as adulterers and be accepted at another church as saints! No wonder so many of our churches are sick. We let infections move around as they spread their deadly viruses (sins) everywhere. It's a deadly yeast spreading through the whole batch of dough.

With regard to fornication, Paul commanded us to "not be deceived." Fornicators are wicked, and they will receive no inheritance in the kingdom of God. Let's see what Paul taught in 1 Corinthians 6:9-11.

YouTube Video: **Having Sex With Your Boyfriend 16**

17

The Deception of Fornication

*"Do you not know that the unrighteous will
not inherit the kingdom of God? Do not be
deceived. Neither fornicators, nor idolaters,
nor adulterers, nor homosexuals, nor
sodomites, nor thieves, nor covetous, nor
drunkards, nor revilers, nor extortioners
will inherit the kingdom of God."*
(1 Corinthians 6:9-10)

The New Testament tells us a lot about deception. It warns us repeatedly that we can be deceived. Using a strong Greek imperative verb of command, Paul told the Corinthians, "Do not be deceived" (6:9). He commanded them later in Chapter 15, "Do not be deceived" (15:33). Paul charged the Galatians, "Do not be deceived" (6:7). James also commanded, "Do not be deceived" (1:16). The apostle John warned, "Let no one deceive you" and that "we can deceive ourselves."[64] When speaking of the last days,

---

[64] See 1 John 3:7 and 1:8.

Jesus also warned, "Take heed that no one deceives you," "take heed that no one deceives you," and again, "take heed that you not be deceived."[65] In his last letter, Paul warned in 2 Timothy 3:13, "Evil men and impostors will grow worse and worse, deceiving and being deceived."

The same Greek word in the New Testament for "deceive" is translated as "going astray." Peter reminds us that "we were like sheep going astray." The wilderness generation was described as "they always go astray in their heart." The apostle reveals that false teachers "have forsaken the right way and gone astray."[66]

The book of Revelation has the greatest revelation of the devil found anywhere in the Bible. John wrote, "The great dragon...that serpent of old, called the Devil and Satan, who deceives the whole world." When he was thrown into the bottomless pit, it was "so that he should deceive the nations no more." As soon as he's released from there, "he will go out to deceive the nations which are in the four corners of the earth." Even as he's cast into the lake of fire, he's described as "the devil, who deceived them." And no wonder, for Jesus said of him, "There is no truth in him. When he speaks a lie, he speaks from his own nature (character), for he is a liar and the father of lies."[67]

The dictionary defines deception as "the practice of deliberately making somebody believe things that are not true; an act, trick, or device intended to deceive or mislead somebody." If I can say it another way, *to deceive someone is to get them to believe a lie.*

Fornication is deceiving. Having sex with your boyfriend is a lie. It's a deception that will send you to hell.

---

[65] See Matthew 24:4; Mark 13:5; and Luke 21:8.

[66] See 1 Peter 2:25; Hebrews 3:10; and 2 Peter 2:15.

[67] See Revelation 12:9, 20:3, 20:8, 20:10; John 8:44.

Here in 1 Corinthians 6:9, Paul asks incredulously, "Do you not know that the unrighteous will not inherit the kingdom of God?" His immediate response is to command them, "Do not be deceived!" Don't let anyone fool you. Don't let people give you sentimental reasons why they've moved in with their girlfriend to save money on rent. Don't let others convince you that everyone is doing it so it can't be that bad. *Don't be deceived.*

Fornication is what unrighteous people do. Fornication will cause a Christian to lose his inheritance in God's kingdom. Don't be deceived.

The apostle then lists ten different types of people who will not inherit God's kingdom (they will go to hell). He writes, "Neither fornicators, nor idolaters, nor adulterers, nor homosexuals, nor sodomites, nor thieves, nor covetous, nor drunkards, nor revilers, nor extortioners will inherit the kingdom of God." Four out of the first five are people involved in sexual sins. Paul says fornicators, adulterers, homosexuals, and sodomites go to hell. This is serious.

We saw in an earlier chapter in this book that fornication is a work of the flesh, and "those who practice such things will not inherit the kingdom of God" (Galatians 5:21). In another chapter, Paul said, "For this you know, that no fornicator...has any inheritance in the kingdom of Christ and God." In the last chapter of this book, we'll see that fornicators "shall have their part in the lake which burns with fire and brimstone, which is the second death" (Revelation 21:8).

Not everything is negative and distressing here in 1 Corinthians Chapter 6. Thankfully, Paul adds, "And such were some of you. But you were washed, but you were sanctified, but you were justified in the name of the Lord Jesus and by the Spirit of our God" (6:11). You *were* like this, but not anymore. You used to be fornicators, but things have changed. Jesus Christ has intervened and all things have been made new. You were washed. Jesus "washed us from our sins in His own blood." "He washed our robes and made them white in the blood of the Lamb." "Christ has sanctified and cleansed us with the washing of water by the word."[68] If you have been fornicating, repent, and be washed by the blood of Jesus. Receive the forgiveness of sins.

Paul continues, "But you were sanctified." Other translations say, "You were made holy." This is an amazing act of God's grace and mercy. Fornicators, adulterers, and homosexuals can be made holy by God. They can be set apart for the Master's use. They can be completely delivered from their corruption and defilement and made holy "by the name of the Lord Jesus and the Spirit of God."

I'll never forget the story of a lady here in our city. As a young Christian teenager, she started dating her boyfriend. Unfortunately, they started having sex and she got pregnant. This caused her a great deal of embarrassment. It brought a lot of shame to her parents and grandparents. Eventually, she repented, got married, and was restored. Today, she is the director of one of the largest para-church ministries here in Fresno. She is perhaps the leading advocate of children born out of wedlock in the Central Valley. "She was washed, sanctified, and justified by Jesus and the Holy Spirit!"

If you are reading this right now and you're fornicating with someone, repent. Don't be deceived. You are not in God's favor. You will not inherit the kingdom of God. However, you can be forgiven, restored, and healed. You can be made new and holy by the power of the Holy Spirit.

---

[68] See Revelation 1:5, 7:14; Ephesians 5:26.

Maybe some people won't like me saying this, but nevertheless, it is true: Nearly all the leaders in our local church were once fornicators. They had children out of wedlock, lived with their girlfriends, or lived a very promiscuous lifestyle before having a personal encounter with the exalted Christ. They have been delivered. They are now some of the most loyal, committed, and faithful church leaders I have ever seen.

One of the most tragic figures in the Bible was Esau, Isaac's firstborn son. The book of Hebrews tells us that all fornicators are just like him. Why is this true? Let's find out in the next chapter.

YouTube Video: **Having Sex With Your Boyfriend 17**

HAVING SEX WITH YOUR BOYFRIEND

18

Fornicators are just like Esau

"Lest there be any fornicator or profane person like Esau, who for one morsel of food sold his birthright. For you know that afterward, when he wanted to inherit the blessing, he was rejected, for he found no place for repentance, though he sought it diligently with tears."
(Hebrews 12:16-17)

Fornicators are just like Esau. They sacrifice a lifetime of future blessings for a few moments for immediate gratification. Esau gave up the incredible blessing of the firstborn male for the ten minutes that he enjoyed a bowl of soup! Fornicators forfeit tremendous blessings from the Lord for the ten minutes they take to have sex with their boyfriends. Instead of maintaining their purity and holiness before God, these fornicating Christians live with a lifetime of shame, guilt, and condemnation. *When you lose your virginity to a boyfriend, you're filled with regret. You can never get that back. It is a terrible burden to carry the rest of your life!* Only in Christ can you experience freedom and forgiveness from this unbearable load of guilt and shame.

Hebrews 12:14-17 must be taken together. Verse 14 ends with a colon (:) and verse 15 with a semicolon (;). And verse 17 is the conclusion of verse 16. Each verse builds upon the previous one. Let's learn some powerful truths about fornication and sexual purity from these important verses in Hebrews.

Hebrews 12:14 – "Pursue peace with all people, and holiness, without which no one will see the Lord." One translation reads, "Make every effort to live in peace with all men and to be holy; without holiness no one will see the Lord." Another ends with these convicting words: "Anyone whose life is not holy will never see the Lord."

If you are dating or courting someone right now, make every effort to live at peace with him/her. Go out of your way to make everything peaceful between you. If you start having sex, you will instantly introduce anxiety, trouble, and turmoil. If you are a Christian, you will lose your peace with God. What a terrible price to pay!

If you start fornicating, you are defiling yourself. You have lost your purity with the Lord. You are walking in darkness and you're going to lose your way in the relationship with your girlfriend. This verse tells us that you're not going to "see the Lord" without holiness. I'm amazed at how many Christians get confused in their relationships once they start fornicating. They become fearful. They are unsettled. Worry and guilt take over as oppressors. Don't live this way. Jesus said, "I am the light of the world. He who follows Me shall not walk in darkness, but have the light of life."[69]

Hebrews 12:15 – "Looking carefully lest anyone fall short of the grace of God; lest any root of bitterness

---

[69] See John 8:12.

springing up cause trouble, and by this many become defiled." I cannot tell you how many young Christian women have told me of the bitterness they felt toward themselves and their boyfriends because they started having sex before marriage. Both of them know it's wrong. Both know they should not have started having sex. The guilt and shame eat at them. Some have gotten pregnant and they had to rush down to the courthouse to get a marriage license and get married right away with the county clerk. That beautiful wedding that they had in mind vanishes into thin air. The images of walking down the aisle to marry prince charming are gone. They become bitter.

The writer of Hebrews tells us that they've fallen short of God's grace. Earlier he had written: "Let us therefore come boldly to the throne of grace, that we may obtain mercy and find grace to help in time of need."[70] God's grace could have kept them from fornicating, but they gave in to the temptation. There is now a seed of resentment that has been planted. It grows into bitterness. As we taught in an earlier chapter, Jesus says that fornication "defiles" a person. Here the author says that "many will be defiled" by this sexual sin. The Greek word there for "defiled" means "to contaminate." Morally, they are tainted.

I remember many years ago a Christian couple who set a date to get married. They asked me to marry them. I agreed. Unfortunately, they started fornicating and she got pregnant. Now, to hide the pregnancy and sexual sin, they moved the date forward. They tried to make it look like she got pregnant on wedding night, but many did the math and the numbers didn't add up. To say the least, there was a lot of fear, shame, and embarrassment.

---

[70] See Hebrews 4:16.

93

Hebrews 12:16 – "Lest there be any fornicator or profane person like Esau, who for one morsel of food sold his birthright." Another says, in part, "...for a single meal sold his inheritance rights..." He gave up his priceless inheritance for a bowl of soup! Fornicators do that too. They lose everything for a moment of pleasure. We become just like Esau. He lost his birthright and his blessing to his deceitful brother.

Hebrews 12:17 has to be the most painful verse on regret in the entire Bible. It says, *"For you know that afterward, when he wanted to inherit the blessing, he was rejected, for he found no place for repentance, though he sought it diligently with tears."* Another translation ends with these distressing words: "It was too late for repentance, even though he begged with bitter tears." Another gives us the heart of the matter – "Esau could find no way to change what he had done."

These are hurtful words – "afterwards," "too late," and "couldn't change what was done." Fornicators cross a line from which there is no return. You cannot get back what you had before. Your innocence is lost. Your virginity is gone. Your purity, peace, and virtue have disappeared. You didn't save yourself for marriage. You cannot undo the damage that has been done.

Too many single Christians live with disappointment, grief, sorrow, and unhappiness. In one brief moment of passion, they become like Esau. They are quickly filled with regret and unbelief. What a heavy burden!

Brothers and sisters in Christ, keep yourself pure. Don't live with regrets; live with confidence. Don't live with shame and bitterness; live with truth and love. Both men and women should come to the altar as virgins. Wait until wedding night. Honor the Lord. Honor your parents and her parents. Don't fornicate and incur all the terrible consequences. Wait patiently for the Lord.

Hebrews 13:4 is the "marriage verse." It tells us that everyone must honor marriage. It also tells us that the one sin that dishonors marriage more than any other is sexual sin. Fornication and adultery defile and tear apart more marriages than anything else. Let's study that verse next.

<u>YouTube Video</u>: **Having Sex With Your Boyfriend 18**

HAVING SEX WITH YOUR BOYFRIEND

19

God will Judge Fornicators

*"Marriage is honorable among all, and the
bed undefiled; but fornicators and
adulterers God will judge."
(Hebrews 13:4)*

I remember a few years ago meeting with a young Christian single who told me in no uncertain terms – "Stop judging me! All Christians are sinners. I'm no worse than anyone else. Why does everyone keep judging me?"

Why did she say these words to me? Because I read five or six verses to her from the Bible on fornication. She was having sex with her boyfriend and I wanted to warn her of the dangers of sexual sin.

There is a great difference between "speaking the truth in love" and "judging one another." If a Christian – any Christian – is committing sexual immorality, it is our Christian responsibility to lovingly tell our brother or sister the truth of God. When we do this, we are not judging them, we are loving them.

Jesus said in John 3:19-21, "Men love darkness rather than light, because their deeds are evil. For everyone practicing evil hates the light and does not come to the light, lest his deeds should be exposed. But he who does the truth comes to the light, that his deeds may be clearly seen, that they have been done in God." When a Christian single is fornicating, he is doing what is evil. He won't come to the light. He is afraid of exposure. He's afraid of being found out. People go into hiding once they start having sex out of wedlock.

Paul spoke of this exposure and why bringing things into the light is so important: "You were once darkness, but now you are light in the Lord. Walk as children of light...and have no fellowship with the unfruitful works of darkness, but rather expose them. For it is shameful even to speak of those things which are done by them in secret. But all things that are exposed are made manifest (revealed) by the light, for whatever makes manifest is light."[71]

Didn't Jesus tell us in Matthew 18:15, "If your brother sins against you, go and tell him his fault between you and him alone. If he hears you, you have gained your brother?"

Wasn't the prophet Ezekiel told, "If you warn the righteous man that the righteous should not sin, and he does not sin, he shall surely live because he took warning; you also will have delivered your soul?"[72] If Ezekiel said nothing out of fear of judging him, God told him that that righteous man would die in his sin and God would hold Ezekiel responsible for his soul. This is serious indeed!

If I see someone driving down a road that leads to a cliff that will result in his death, it is the height of irresponsibility if I say nothing for fear of offending him.

Paul told us that we should be "warning every man and teaching every man in all wisdom, that we may present every man perfect in Christ Jesus."[73]

---

[71] See Ephesians 5:8, 11-13.

[72] See Ezekiel 3:21.

[73] See Colossians 1:28.

Paul also wrote in 1 Thessalonians 5:14, "Warn those who are unruly." Warning someone is not the same as judging someone. As I approach some train tracks, and a train is coming at a high rate of speed, I really appreciate the lowering of the warning gates and the flashing red lights. *The train operators are not critiquing my driving; they are warning me of a deadly situation if I don't stop!* I'm being warned, not judged.

When it comes to fornication, we shouldn't be too worried about man's judgment, but we should definitely be concerned about God's judgment. Hebrews 13:4 states clearly that *God will judge all fornicators and adulterers.* Let's look carefully at this powerful verse and see what we can learn.

This verse in Hebrews tells us three very important truths about marriage and sex within marriage:

"Marriage is honorable among all." Another translation says, "Marriage should be honored by everyone." Still another says, "Marriage should be honored by all." One says simply, "Give honor to marriage."

All Christians must honor marriage. The Greek word here for "honor" means "valuable; highly esteemed." It is actually translated in some other verses as "dear" or "most precious." Guthrie writes, "Marriage should be esteemed as of great worth."[74] Whatever any culture honors, people will aspire to it. If we elevate and honor marriage, young people will desire to find a future husband or wife and marry. This is honorable.

This verse also tells me that nothing else dishonors and disgraces marriage like sexual sin. The worst injury anyone can inflict on the marriage institution

---

[74] *Hebrews*, George H. Guthrie, The NIV Application Commentary, Zondervan Publishers, Grand Rapids, Michigan, page 436.

is by committing sexual immorality. It's an act of betrayal. It violates our trust in the most profound way.

When you save yourself for marriage, you are honoring marriage. There is great glory in coming to the wedding altar as a virgin. Don't dilute the power of your marriage vows by mixing in the corrupting influence of sexual immorality.

Save yourself for the one you will love forever!

The second part of the verse is very important. It reads, "Keep the bed undefiled." Another translation says, "The marriage bed must be kept pure."

The Greek word here for "bed" is "koitē." This was a piece of furniture like "a couch" where a man and a woman "cohabited." It is where we get the technical English term for sexual intercourse, "coitus." It comes from a Latin word, "coire," which means literally "go together."

The author of Hebrews says that sexual intercourse must be "undefiled" or literally "not tainted or not contaminated." One Greek dictionary defines the word as "unsoiled." It's interesting to me that the word used here for "undefiled" or "pure" (amiantos) "is the same word used in Hebrews 7:26 to describe the holiness of Christ our high priest."[75] You can't get any purer than that!

The only sex that is pure in God's eyes is between a married man and his wife. When you fornicate or commit adultery, you are defiling God's marriage covenant. We are desecrating something that God considers holy. We are vomiting over something God wants pure. Again, Jesus said that fornication begins in the heart and it "defiles a man." Sexual sin defiles marriage.

---

[75] See *Hebrews*, Donald A. Hagner, New International Biblical Commentary, Hendrickson Publishers, Peabody, Massachusetts, page 236.

"*Fornicators (pornos) and adulterers God will judge*." The NLT says, "God will surely judge people who are immoral and those who commit adultery." Another says, "God will punish anyone who is immoral or unfaithful in marriage."

This truth must be taught by all Christians everywhere. Never forget it: GOD WILL JUDGE FORNICATORS. Even if no one else knows; even if no one else confronts you; even if you're secretly fornicating with your boyfriend, know for sure – *you will be judged by God.* You might reject the judgment of men, but you cannot avoid the judgment of God. God will judge you even if no one else will. I recall here those fearful words from the lips of Jesus in Luke 12:4-5: "My friends, do not be afraid of those who kill the body, and after that have no more that they can do. But I will show you whom you should fear: Fear Him who, after He has killed, has power to cast into hell; yes, I say to you, fear Him!"

I don't know all that is involved with God judging someone, but it surely cannot be good. Just a few chapters earlier, the writer of Hebrews wrote, "There is only the terrible expectation of God's judgment...Just think how much worse the punishment will be for those who have trampled on the Son of God, and have treated the blood of the covenant, which made us holy, as if it were common and unholy, and have insulted and disdained the Holy Spirit who brings God's mercy to us. For we know the One who said, 'I will take revenge; I will pay them back.' He also said, 'The Lord will judge His own people.' It is a terrible thing to face punishment from the living God."[76] Many Christians say that God never judges His people. But these verses above say clearly that "the Lord will judge *His own people*." Throughout the Bible, God punished and disciplined those who disobeyed His

---

[76] See Hebrews 10:27-31, NLT.

commands and laws. Let us never make light of God's judgments! Let us never make excuses for our sins and compromises. Augustine said, "Listen here to what God is saying, not to what your own prejudice is saying in favor of your sins, or to your friend, perhaps, chained with the same shackles of wickedness as yourself – though in fact he is more your enemy and his own."[77]

The next chapter teaches us about the final judgment of God. We'll go to Revelation to see that fornicators, if they do not repent, they will be cast into the lake of fire.

YouTube Video: **Having Sex With Your Boyfriend 19**

---

[77] *Hebrews*, Ancient Christian Commentary on Scripture, Volume X, Edited by Erik M. Heen and Philip D. W. Krey, InterVarsity Press, Downers Grove, Illinois, page 230.

20

Fornicators in the Lake of Fire

"But the cowardly, unbelieving,
abominable, murderers, sexually immoral,
sorcerers, idolaters, and all liars shall have
their part in the lake which burns with fire
and brimstone, which is the second death."
(Revelation 21:8)

The phrase, "lake of fire," is found five times in the Bible with all occurrences in the Book of Revelation (See 19:20, 20:11-15, 21:7-8, 21:27, and 22:14-15). The lake of fire is the "everlasting fire" spoken of by Jesus. It is the place of "eternal punishment" where the "fire is never quenched" and "the worm never dies." It is the most terrifying of all places for the wicked dead.

There are at least five basic and fearful truths about the lake of fire found in the Book of Revelation and other associated verses in the New Testament. In proper order, they are:

- *It is a lake:* It is not a desert; it is not a mountain; it is not a river; it is not a spring, nor is it an ocean.

It is a lake. In the natural, a lake is a large body of water surrounded by land. It is not moving or free-flowing. It is stationary. Most people think of a lake as a place that has cool, fresh water. Tourists usually take pictures of lakes. Lakes are beautiful. However, the lake of fire is a place of torment. It is not beautiful; it is terrible. No one will take pictures here for it is a place of utter darkness!

- *It is a lake of fire:* It is not a lake of water; it is a lake of fire. Here is the wording from Revelation – "the lake of *fire*...," "the lake of *fire*...," "the lake of *fire*...," "the lake of *fire*...," and "the lake which *burns* with *fire*..." This is the eternal fire of hell.

- *It is a lake of fire and brimstone:* Chemically, brimstone is the same as sulfur. It is a yellow-orange color. Brimstone is "the stone that is burning" (on fire). It's the Old English word, "byrne," which means "burning." Biblically, "brimstone" was an element used in God's judgments. Notice how the Book of Revelation describes it: "These two were cast alive into the lake of fire burning with *brimstone*" (19:20), "the devil, who deceived them, was cast into the lake of fire and *brimstone*" (20:10), "...the lake which burns with fire and *brimstone*" (21:8), and "he shall be tormented with fire and *brimstone* in the presence of the holy angels and in the presence of the Lamb" (14:10).

- *The lake of fire is the second death:* If there is a "second" death, then there has to be a first death. The first death is physical; the second death is spiritual. In the first, you are separated from your body; in the second, you are separated from the Lord (forever). The phrase, "second death," is found only in Revelation. Revelation 20:14, "Then Death and Hades were cast into the lake of fire. This is the *second death*." Revelation 21:8, "...the lake which burns with fire and brimstone, which is the *second death*." Only true, born-again believers escape the second death: "He who has an ear, let him hear what the Spirit says to the churches. He who overcomes shall not be hurt by the *second death*" and "blessed and holy is he who has part in the first resurrection. Over such the *second death* has no power, but they shall be priests of God and of Christ, and shall reign with Him a thousand years."[78] We want to be part of the "first resurrection," not the "second death!"

- *It is a lake of torment:* The lake of fire is a place of torment (agony), outer darkness, and weeping and gnashing of teeth. John wrote in Revelation 20:10, "And they will be *tormented* day and night forever and ever" and Revelation 14:10-11, "He shall be *tormented* with fire...and the smoke of their *torment* ascends forever and ever."[79]

Both Revelation 21:8 and 22:15 show us that fornicators are cast into this lake of fire – "But the cowardly, unbelieving, abominable, murderers, *sexually immoral* (pornois), sorcerers, idolaters, and all liars shall have their part in the lake which burns with fire and brimstone, which is the second death" and "but outside (of the New Jerusalem) are dogs and sorcerers and *sexually immoral* (pornoi) and murderers and idolaters, and whoever loves and practices a lie."

---

[78] See Revelation 2:11 and 20:6.

[79] All of the teaching here on the lake of fire was taken from my book, *The Christian and Hell*, available on Amazon. See pages 19-23.

This truth was already taught by Paul in 1 Corinthians 6:9-10, Galatians 5:21, and Ephesians 5:3-7 when he wrote that no fornicators will ever inherit the kingdom of God and of Christ.

Not only are fornicators found in the lake of fire, but also all unrepentant murderers, sorcerers, liars, and idolaters. Every unbeliever and hateful person who ever lived will be found there – forever! The devil, the beast, the false prophet, Judas, all the wicked angels, and every evil person go to this lake. Even "Death and Hades were cast into the lake of fire."[80]

Every unrepentant, sexually immoral man and woman who was a pimp, adulterer, homosexual, lesbian, and child molester will be together forever in the lake of fire! What a horrific reality!

Revelation 20:15 summarizes who will be there: "And anyone not found written in the Book of Life was cast into the lake of fire." Only those who have found salvation in Christ Jesus and His work on the cross will be delivered from this terrible lake. Earlier, Jesus had told the Sardis church, "He who overcomes shall be clothed in white garments, and I will not blot out his name from the Book of Life; but I will confess his name before My Father and before His angels."[81] We want to make sure our names are in the Lamb's Book of Life! Later, John describes those who can and can't enter into the New Jerusalem, the city of the living God: "But there shall by no means enter it anything that defiles, or causes an abomination or a lie, but only those who are written in the Lamb's Book of Life." Fornication defiles, and it shuts people out of God's heavenly home.

We examined Hebrews 13:4 in our last chapter – "God will judge fornicators and adulterers." The lake of fire is the last and ultimate judgment for sexual sin.

---

[80] See Revelation 20:14.
[81] See Revelation 3:5.

All around the world today, people, including Christians, are corrupting themselves with sexual immorality. People are viewing pornography, lusting, fornicating with boyfriends, committing adultery, having affairs, and engaging in homosexuality and lesbianism. These people often condemn Christians who speak out against sexual sin. We are labelled as bigots and judgmental. Today, there is no fear of God or His judgments. But the lake of fire is a fearful reality. The lake of fire stands as a powerful reminder of what God thinks of sexual immorality. No one gets away unpunished with fornication. Fornicators experience devastating consequences here on earth and eternal consequences after their life is over. Yet, people mock at God's judgments and the truth of God. This is no laughing matter. The lake of fire should put a great fear of God in all of us. God is not playing games. Neither should we.

YouTube Video: **Having Sex With Your Boyfriend 20**

HAVING SEX WITH YOUR BOYFRIEND

CHAPTER 1:
- Using your own words, write a definition for "fornication" as you understand it.
- How can the apostle Paul say that "fornicating" is "acting just like a prostitute?" How does this definition confirm its evil nature?
- What did Jesus say about prostitutes in Matthew 21:31-32?

CHAPTER 2:
- What did Jesus mean in Matthew 15:19-20 when He said that "fornication" (along with other sins) "defiles you?"
- The author, quoting 2 Timothy 2:20-21, states that unclean vessels cannot be used by the Master (Jesus). Why is this true?
- How can we conclude that "evil actions" come from "evil thoughts" in Mark 7:21-22? Compare with Genesis 6:5.

CHAPTER 3:
- Using your own words, define what temptation is. What is the best way to deal with any temptation?
- Why is "fleeing fornication" a sign of strength, not weakness?
- Read the story of Joseph and Potiphar's wife in Genesis 39. What are some important lessons here about sexual temptation?

CHAPTER 4:
- Should having sex be one of the main reasons for getting married? Are there other priorities?
- What did Paul mean in 1 Corinthians 7:9 when he said, "It is better to marry than to burn?"

- Why should kissing and touching (especially excessive) be avoided with boyfriends and girlfriends?

CHAPTER 5:
- Jesus is Lord over your body. What does that mean practically?
- Summarize what Jesus did with His body in Hebrews 10:5-10.
- The author says a glove is for the hand, and Paul said food was for the stomach. What does this have to do with the argument in this chapter?

CHAPTER 6:
- In your own words, what is repentance? How does a Christian repent of his sins?
- According to 2 Corinthians 12:21, how did Paul react when Christians did not repent of fornication?
- What begins to happen in people's lives who continue to fornicate and not repent?

CHAPTER 7:
- What does it mean that sexual immorality is a work of the flesh?
- According to Paul in Galatians 5 and Romans 8, how does a Christian win the war against the flesh and lust?
- On a practical level, how does a believer "put to death the deeds of the body" (Romans 8:13)?

CHAPTER 8:
- What exactly did Paul mean in Ephesians 5:5 when he wrote that fornicators would not inherit the kingdom of Christ?

- Why do you think that there is so much deception about fornication in our culture and in the church?
- Do you think a Christian can be a "son of disobedience" in Ephesians 5:6 and Colossians 3:6? Why or why not?

CHAPTER 9:
- What exactly does it mean that you are "dead to sin" and that you "died with Christ?"
- What does it mean that sexual sin works through your members?
- What are some practical things you can do to "put fornication to death in your members?"

CHAPTER 10:
- What does it mean that God did not call us to uncleanness, but to holiness? See 1 Thessalonians 4:7.
- Do you agree with the author that many fornicators become adulterers? Why or why not?
- What exactly does it mean that "the Lord is the avenger of all such" in 1 Thessalonians 4:6?

CHAPTER 11:
- Why can the author state that sexual sins are the most devastating and the most prevalent in our society today?
- Why do you think God chose to depict Babylon as a "prostitute" who corrupted the kings and inhabitants of the earth with "her fornication?"
- In practical terms, what does it mean to "come out of Babylon" so we don't participate in her plagues? See Revelation 18:4-6.

CHAPTER 12:
- Why do you think people, including Christians, are so stubborn and unwilling to repent of sexual immorality (even though it is destroying their lives?"
- What were both "Balaam" and "Jezebel" bringing into the church that resulted in so much sexual immorality?
- What is Jesus teaching us in Revelation 2:23?

CHAPTER 13:
- Balaam could not curse Israel from the outside, but he did from the inside. How did he do this according to Numbers 31:16?
- As you read 1 Corinthians 10:6-10, how are these Old Testament stories "examples" (verses 6, 11) for us today?
- Read Numbers Chapter 25. What truths stand out to you?

CHAPTER 14:
- Why is it today that if you stand against sexual immorality, you're considered narrow-minded, a bigot, or a hater?
- Why did the early apostles highlight "fornication" or "sexual immorality" in their letters to new Christians?
- In practical terms, what does "abstinence" mean regarding sexual sin?

CHAPTER 15:
- Exactly how and why are "your bodies the members of Christ" in 1 Corinthians 6:15?
- What kind of spiritual and emotional confusion was Solomon living with having sex with over 1,000 women? See 1 Kings 11:3.

- While quoting Genesis 2:24, Paul says that a man "who is joined to a harlot becomes one body with her." What does he mean?

CHAPTER 16:
- Is handing someone over to Satan for sexual immorality too harsh? How exactly should the church deal with this? See 1 Corinthians 5:4-5.
- Paul told us to judge and "put out evil persons" from our fellowship for sexual sin. How do we reconcile this instruction with Jesus' command not to judge others? See 1 Corinthians 5:12-13 and Matthew 7:1-5?
- Exactly what did Paul mean in 1 Corinthians 5:6 that "a little leaven leavens the whole lump?"

CHAPTER 17:
- What is so deceiving about sexual sin?
- What does Paul mean in 1 Corinthians 6:9 that "the unrighteous will not inherit the kingdom of God?" What will they inherit?
- Can you tell the testimony of someone today who was once a fornicator, adulterer, or homosexual but who is now serving the Lord? See 1 Corinthians 6:11.

CHAPTER 18:
- What begins to happen to Christian singles once they start fornicating? Their peace with God and one another? Their purity?
- How exactly are fornicators just like Esau?
- What are some of the regrets that Christian singles live with after committing sexual immorality?

CHAPTER 19:
- Why does fornication and adultery dishonor marriage more than all other sins?
- What begins to happen in the life of a fornicator who is under God's judgment? What happened to David after he committed adultery with Bathsheba? See 2 Kings Chapter 11-13.
- What does Hebrews 10:26-31 tell us about God's judgments?

CHAPTER 20:
- In your own words, describe the lake of fire.
- Why should the prospect of being cast into the lake of fire be our greatest deterrent against sexual sin?
- In your own words, define the eight different types of people who will be thrown into the lake of fire in Revelation 21:8.

About the Author

Charlie Avila is the Senior Pastor of Clovis Christian Center in Fresno, California. He is married to Irma and has two adult children – Leah (husband: Jose) and Daniel. Pastor Charlie is the Bible teacher of the Spirit of Wisdom and Revelation teaching newsletters and the principal teacher on the Teacher of the Bible website.

He is an instructor with the Fresno School of Mission and other ministry schools. He has spoken in conferences locally, nationally, and internationally. He teaches special seminars on various Bible subjects and verse by verse studies through Old Testament and New Testament books. He has written several books available on Amazon including *The Christian and Anger*, *The Christian and Homosexuality*, *The Christian and Hell*, *The Christian & Witchcraft*, *Detecting & Dealing with False Teachings*, *Healing the Sick*, *How to Become a Christian*, *The End Times*, *Making Disciples One on One*, *Having Sex with Your Boyfriend*, *Witnessing to Jehovah's Witnesses* and various commentaries on books of the Bible including Esther, 2 Peter, and Jude. He also has many books in Spanish by the same titles as the English versions.

He can be contacted at teacherofthebible@gmail.com or Clovis Christian Center, 3606 N. Fowler Ave, Fresno, CA 93727-1124.

The videos teachings for each chapter of this book are available on YouTube. Just type "Having Sex with Your Boyfriend Pastor Charlie Avila" on the search line or type "teacher of the Bible" and subscribe. The videos are also available at www.teacherofthebible.com.

HAVING SEX WITH YOUR BOYFRIEND

Scriptural Reference Index

Made in the USA
Las Vegas, NV
19 April 2022

47691001R00075